LIFE MANAGEMEN'

MW01144668

THE
ART AND SCIENCE OF
MINDFULNESS

Encounters with Nothingness

Parminder Sohal (Yog Nanak)
BSc, MBA, EI Coach & Meditatoin Facilitator

978-1-7344866-3-6 (Paperback)

978-1-7344866-4-3 (Ebook)

978-1-7344866-5-0 (Audio)

book interior and cover design by

Hammad Khalid

www.HMDgfx.com

"When you love someone, the most precious gift you can give your loved one is your true presence and awaken in them their own presence."
- Yog Nanak

EDITOR'S PREFACE

The experience of editing this book has taught me so much. Generally, my perception has been influenced; from processing pain to dealing with pain, and on so many subjects that were highlighted thus.

This book is meant for anyone who is looking for a different approach to life. The whole idea of mindfulness is being more aware of our current experiences, with the ability to totally accept our reality or a way to relate with our inner consciousness or mind. Mindfulness practice is also a trustworthy pathway to ensure we have a heightened level of wisdom, fulfillment and compassion in our lives.

According to the author, mindfulness is known to be a "process" and not a "function". It is a process which seeks ways to alter relationships. These relationships are of differing nature in relation to our thoughts, and we can often carry them out in our daily lives without knowing them or being conscious of them. The most notable trigger for these practices, for most people, is during tough times.

Parminder further goes to explain that the idea of mindfulness can influence all aspects of our being; from the structure of our brain to our character etc. Though it has also become an established fact, through adequate studies, that mindfulness can assist in alleviating a broad range of psychological difficulties such as depression, addictions, interpersonal problems, anxiety and even problems associated with aging, the writer balances this out, by highlighting that mindfulness is not the solution to every problem.

There are several practices involved in mindfulness as stated by the author, but one most worthy of note is Meditation. From the relationship between attention and empathy to the science of self-compassion, all the topics discussed in the book had this common denomination; meditation.

The writer ends by sharing some of the benefits of meditation which includes; regulation of mood and anxiety disorders, decreases depression, improves psychomotor vigilance and may decrease sleep need, reduce panic disorder, increase the grey matter in the brain and so on.

Quite noteworthy is the passion of the writer, his grammatical inference and general composition in delivering the message showed to a great degree his level of passion for the subject. As a result of his adequate composure in writing, editing this book was quite intuitive, impacting and superfluous. He ended by recommending a home for proper mindfulness practices, which from all indications, is a home indeed. This book is a worthy read, and I highly recommend it.

Lisa Newman,

President, Victoria Rental and Relocation Services,

Victoria, BC, Canada.

CONTENTS

CHAPTER ONE;

THE SCIENCE OF
MINDFULNESS

"Techniques are helpful because they are scientific. You are saved from unnecessary wandering, unnecessary groping; if you don't know any techniques, you will take a long time."
~OSHO

The state of Mindfulness is the degree of awareness of your current experiences, an ability to accept a simple manner, or a way of relating with the constituents of your inner consciousness or mind. This has been positively and productively practiced in alleviating physical suffering to enhance emotional well-being. It has been in practice for a period of 2,500 years, even before the existence of Buddha.

The validity of what we have been taught and nurtured to believe, by ancient wisdom over thousands of years, is currently and constantly being validated and proven to be true and essential through the continuous advancement of technology and scientific research. It is well stated that the ability to practice mindfulness is the most effective solution to the innate propensity we as humans have for psychological distress.

Mindfulness practice is also a trustworthy pathway to ensure we have a heightened level of wisdom, fulfillment, and compassion in our lives.

The brain structure is also confirmed to become affected by mindfulness. Neurobiologists have clearly stated that precise changes are notable in meaningful and desirable ways. With this, other mental health professionals are going a step further to discover the riches and level of promise mindfulness bodes for other aspects of human lives.

To this, they see promise in how much impact mindfulness can be, not only to personal development but as a tool to bring together and drive forward every facet of psychotherapy.

It has also become an established fact, through adequate studies, that mindfulness can assist in alleviating a broad range of psychological difficulties such as depression, addictions, interpersonal problems, anxiety and even problems associated with aging. However, this isn't to say that mindfulness is a perfect fit or an absolute solution to every problem out there.

Depending on the degree of needs, or individual predicaments, mindfulness practices have to be selectively tweaked to meet each need. In addition, mindfulness can only be successfully inculcated into our personal lives via intuitive and visceral understanding of what it means to practice it, without neglecting the intellectual aspect as well.

Therefore, to reap the proceeds of mindfulness, we must first learn to practice it effectively. To do this, we need to ask ourselves an important question;

WHAT IS MINDFULNESS?

In relation to Western Psychotherapy and Neuroscience, "Mindfulness" is gotten in translation from the word "Sati," which was in turn gotten from the ancient language called "Pali". Pali happens to be the language of the Buddha because it was what his teachings were spoken in.

Sati denotes and encourages awareness, a sense of attention and the need to always remember. It also bears a sense of "non-judgment" to the enterprise of humanity as a whole, a deep level of acceptance regardless of the level of circumstances, and a soothing form of friendliness based on kindness.

Mindfulness is made of three essential components, *one* of which is *"awareness of the current experience with absolute acceptance."*

In our modern times, mindfulness practices have gone global and are rapidly becoming mainstream psychotherapy, so much so that people are now attempting to measure it through constructed scales. We are often too distracted by things of the past or future that our mind doesn't dally in the current moment. Yet, those moments which are most important to us are the situations in which our mind is present.

Yet, we continually waste precious time in memories and fantasies of the past and future respectively.

It is also noteworthy that people get trapped in different levels or domains in their consciousness. It is why you would have people compare themselves to others in a different light. For instance, some value the comparisons on who is wealthier, while others go for who is smarter and so on. This abject regard for ranking, in the primate beings, manifests itself in humans as a whole in relation with how we always want to measure ourselves to others.

These are some of the things mindfulness practices can assist us with. It will and can assist us in acknowledging and accepting things for what they are and seeing them as such, rather than what they can be or what we wish them to be desperately. This means that they can assist us in dealing with the inevitable aspects of life; death and illness.

Mindfulness also assists in casting off any form of judgmental beliefs we might have about others. It brings clarity of mind towards others. In so doing, we are able to take things with ease and not get emotionally triggered by the slightest things. When this occurs, it becomes apparent to us that our characters as individuals are the consequence of whatever disturbing behavior the others exhibit.

"Mindfulness can help reflect our own current struggles"

Relationships can benefit from mindfulness practices too. They are essential in assisting us to be more empathic and supportive towards others and their plights. It is only with mindfulness that we can work with others through hard times. It also curbs obsessive or compulsive acts and replaces that aspect of us with thoughtfulness and calm when we want to act.

Mindfulness Practices and Scientific Findings

Facets of science such as neuroscience, psychology, and medicine are just a few of the mainstream where mindfulness practices are now being inculcated into. Mindfulness in relation to how it positively affects the body, mind, and brain, is now being studied by the aforementioned facets of science.

Apart from how it prevents our brain from aging, mindfulness activates certain brain circuits linked to emotions such as happiness, becoming energized and much more. They are also known to lengthen telomeres; the ends of chromosomes that become worn with stress which subsequently leads to aging through cell death.

To experienced students who are versed in the study of mindfulness, it is strange that a millimeter of change in brain tissue, as depicted by an MRI, or a sudden alteration in EEG activity generates more belief in current times than the age-old reports handed down from generations of people such as monks and nuns. These people had indulged in these practices and used them to execute peace, fulfillment and even wellness for thousands of years.

To those who are newbies to mindfulness practices, scientific findings and evaluations are essential in regards to the tenacity of abstract religious, medical and philosophical claims through the ages.

Those who have indulged in mindfulness practices, and also have happened to teach them to others, must embrace the simple fact that what science is now doing is validating time-honored practices and observations about the power of mindfulness.

This point was where my journey began; when I was diagnosed with a brain hemorrhage, but was still able to walk out of the hospital after three days. I did this by remaining and thriving in a meditative state; this changed the frame of science in regards to mindfulness for me. In retrospect, it is important to note that "Science" is a latin word which means "Knowing".

In lieu of all of these, how about we step onward in our journey and voyage through these mindfulness practices together?

How to Become More Mindful

Mindfulness is known to be a "process" and not a "function". It is a process that seeks for ways to alter relationships. These relationships are of differing nature in relation to our thoughts, and we can often carry them out in our daily lives without knowing them or being conscious of them. The most notable trigger for these practices, for most people, is during tough times.

Practicing mindfulness shatters the archaic practices; this means that sometimes, in some ways, hardship can become a blessing as well.

Notably, even while these are called "Mindfulness practices," they are practices related with the body and mind functioning as one. This is simply because they take note of our experiences in consciousness as they are being derived from our body and mind. It is a culmination practice of "Yoga" which means union between your body and mind, and it creates the possibility for one to be able to listen to the duo at the same time and not apart.

Yoga isn't in any way gymnastics, and meditation isn't all about zoning out and concentrating, but rather, it is the ability to gain clarity and see things as they ought to be seen. It is far richer, deeper and more profound, and we are going to explore the entire process together.

There are three important skills we are going to take note of, learn about, and also develop under the coverage of mindfulness practices and we will seek some assistance from neurobiologists in clarifying them.

The first skill is centered on the rationally termed concentration, which in actuality is *"Attention"*.

The second skill is what neurobiologists call *"Open Monitoring,"* which was known to be choice-less awareness or even mindfulness in the "Zen Tradition". Don't worry about this, because I know how confusing it can be. It was not until the introduction of mindfulness practices to the west that people began to use the umbrella term "Mindfulness" to shelter a number of different sub-practices.

Notably, open monitoring is implored to observe and note how the mind creates suffering for itself.

The third skill is *"Acceptance and Loving Kindness"*. This is typically used to soothe and provide comfort.

The neurobiological evidence provided states that the individual mental skill cultivated by these three different meditation types represents, though with rather distinct and precise processes, degrees of overlapping in the brain.

For instance, in your bid to become a photographer, your first lesson would be amassing the skill on how to focus the lens. Without that skill locked down, you are bound to become limited to impressionism. Yet, if you successfully lockdown that skill, you will have to master the art of taking pictures of anything. This is no different from the manner in which we use focused attention to refine the attention of the mind and train it to see what is occurring around it in each moment.

When this is done, we can then successfully open the mind to what arises in awareness, so we can see for ourselves how it creates suffering or misery for itself.

Points to Reflect on

- What time or moments of your day have you found yourself to be most mindful?
- What time or moments of your day have you found yourself to be mindless or lost in thoughts?
- Can you reflect on such moments in which your mind makes comparisons between yourself and another entity? On what basis does your mind do this?
- Are you aware of how you are losing your time and life, and would you like to be a little more effective to be able to live your life?
- If so, what things do you need the most to begin this journey?

Notes for Reflection

CHAPTER TWO

HOW TO DO INFORMAL, FORMAL AND INTENSIVE MEDITATION PRACTICES

"Meditation is not a method; it is not simply a technique. You cannot learn it. It is a growth: a growth of your total living, out of your total living. Meditation is not something that can be added to you as you are. It cannot be added to you; it can only come to you through a basic transformation, a mutation. It is a flowering, a growth. Growth is always from the total; it is not an addition. Just like love, it cannot be added to you. It grows out of you, out of your totality. You must grow towards meditation."
~ OSHO

Being "Vs." Doing

Mindfulness can be simply related with acquiring the ability to handle a musical instrument, because it too, is a dose-related activity. With a little bit of practice, we can attain and develop a little bit of mindfulness as well. It, therefore, translates that doing more mindful activity will inevitably develop your mindfulness some more.

This form of "experience-dependent" neuroplasticity is the manner in which our brain fibers attain girth when we indulge and use them over and over and again. Donald Tabb, a great and renowned neurobiologist once said, *"Neurons that fire together, wire together."*

It, therefore, goes to say that every mindfulness practice involves the art of "being". This is somewhat unknown to most of us because we are more involved and indulged in the constant focus of "doing". As a result of the fear associated with falling behind, which most of us have, we constantly try to stay afloat of situations and things we need to get done.

It is hard for many of us to live in the present because; simply "being" channels our mind to unwanted thoughts and emotions. It is a natural act for us to constantly defend ourselves against, or to cast off these unpleasant thoughts and emotions from our sense of awareness.

We fail to realize that we need to actually sit and pay attention to be able to realize mindfulness for what it is; a means to cultivate awareness of present or current experience and as a result, develop the ability to accept it. It becomes very hard to do this because everything in these current times moves at a maddening pace. Therefore, I encourage you to think of mindfulness, not as multi-tasking or juggling different things at once, as single-tasking.

Cognitive scientists argued against the notion that people can multitask with their analogy that likened attention to a pie. In attempting to carry out two things at once, your attention is split into fifty-fifty between the two. If you attempt four at the same time, you'll split your attention into twenty-five percent each, and so on.

How Can We Meditate in Our Busy Lives?

Mindfulness practices emphasize, in teaching us, how delay is inevitable with hurry. It means for every time you attempt to hurry, you invariably cause a delay. Some options for meditation practices include;

- **Formal Meditation Practice;** this is a specific time set aside from your day to consciously develop your sense of mindfulness with specific resources.
- **Informal Meditation Practice;** these are things; we partake in during the course of our busy day that develops some sense of mindfulness.
- **Intensive Retreat Practice;** this is when we choose to practice mindfulness somewhere away from our normal loci, over a period of a few selected days and time.

An apt example is the "telephone meditation"; a common practice in today's busy periods. How do you do this? Well, it is simple; first tweak your call settings so your phone does not activate the response from you when a call comes through. When the phone rings, let it ring for few times, take a moment to breathe, pause and listen to it ring for a while.

Sit there, amass the sound of the ringing telephone and, in that moment, grant your mind the ability to focus your attention on what is going on presently in the moment. While you do this, allow your attention to be fixated on something that will bring you back into awareness of present experiences with a degree of acceptance.

With the growth of technology, we now have cell phones, with "Caller ID," which has enhanced the chances for us to meditate. We first pick up the sound from the ringing phone before noticing the number calling us, before we feel and experience any emotional response in relation to that number calling.

Judging by this experience, it is safe to say we have different associations and emotional responses to numbers, and with each number popping up on our screen comes a degree of varying emotional responses coursing through our bodies.

Asides phone calls, mindful practices can also be carried out during driving. By turning off the radio which often occupies our attention, we can streamline our focus on the sounds from traffic, and sights associated with everything around us; nature and the environment. It is even better when you're driving a manual car. This also assists in bringing us profound attention to the moment and the environment.

We can also engage in mindfulness during activities such as dog walking, walking to and from our car, waiting on the bus and even while we wait in line. All we need to prevent ourselves from doing, during these periods, is getting tempted to check our smartphones every thirty seconds. In fact, it is best we abstain from our phone entirely.

Any activity that can help us single-task and be present in "a moment" is an opportunity for an informal form of mindfulness practice, and we should encourage it.

To be able to attain the next level in mindfulness, we must be willing to partake in some formal meditation. I often conduct three days meditation, from fridays to sundays; this way it bears no impact on work or other intense meditation which we carry out during the 7 days and 21 days in OSHO meditation centers, and in other ashrams around the world.

By so doing, we must also recognize the fact that we need protected environments and lab-conditioned locations that can fully take you into deep experience and awareness.

Neurologists have conclusively studied that people who are involved in a lot of meditation practices develop more robust structures in certain areas of their brains. Since the cerebral cortex thins as we age; this is of benefit to us.

Based on research carried out, in Mass General Hospital in Boston, between people who have been meditating for years against those who haven't of the same age and of similar life circumstances, it was found that several areas of the brain, compared to those who actively meditated, deteriorated in the non-meditators.

It has been conclusively proven by scientists that when people undergo certain positive emotional responses, there is a great deal of left prefrontal activation. In difference, when they experience negative emotional responses, there is more profound activation in their right prefrontal region.

With all these said about mindfulness, it is also worthy to note that mindfulness practices aren't all about allowance.

"Mindfulness practices involves restraint."

Mindfulness practices in no way preach asceticism or the need to scrub off desires, but instead, they demand that we perform naturally while taking time to focus on what is ongoing in the present.

For those who are lucky enough to engage in breath awareness training, you must have noticed that you don't even act on an itch or an ache whenever you experience it. This is the same for those who have been to weeklong vipassana meditation. When you don't act on this itch, it might be because, in that present moment, you believe the itch or the ache will transform by itself.

This is very similar to a lot of other things. For instance, though we don't always act on anger, even when we see it fueling and rising, we notice it transforming by itself. This is what mindfulness practices help us do; realizing that we have choices on whether or not to act on impulses. That particular holdback against acting is an important aspect in utilizing mindfulness practices when we work with a host of psychological and behavioral difficulties.

These difficulties might range from anxieties to addictions, to stress-related and induced medical disorders and so on.

An intensive retreat is also advised for those who intend to up their mindfulness practice level. In this retreat, you will be able to go off and spend several days out in nature, simply performing mindfulness practices each day. The most basic rule during this period is to retreat out in nature. Also, the practice of talking or checking of cellphones should not be allowed.

During this period, eye contact shouldn't be allowed or even be a thing, and the eyes should be locked unto what is called "noble silence".

Why is this done?

Well, the reason behind this practice is to develop sufficient concentration for open monitoring skills to enable the mind to notice what is going on in its environment at the moment.

In relation to this period, the mind experiences different things. One of these experiences it battles with is a concept of psychoanalysis called "transference". Transference means the inability to see people as a reflection of other people and what those people remind us of, and not what they are in particular.

The mind is quite powerful and it has the ability to create stories about people we have minimal data about in such a grand manner that it feels like reality, and this is based on the things we see these people doing. It is easier to say the mind begins to weave an elaborate or profound ideology about others based on bits and little information it amasses.

Walking and Eating Meditation

Walking meditation is mostly practiced during retreats so that the body and mind don't begin to feel stiff or restricted. It is wonderful to practice because it does not have any formal restrictions. There are a host of benefits aligned with walking meditation and they include; an ability to easily transform from a formal meditation to an informal one, and the opportunity to be mindful whenever we are walking.

Eating meditation also has no formal restrictions. It can function in both formal and informal ways. In terms of being mindful of what we are eating, it is similar to walking meditation. It is also very essential when our mind is distracted because the art of eating is a vivid object of awareness and stimulus, where we can easily avert our focus on food when or if the mind is unsettled.

When we take our time to eat slowly, we tend to notice that as the food crosses through to the duodenum, a signal is reverted back to the hypothalamus which tell us of a degree of satiation occurring. This translates into us having had enough to eat. For many of us who consume large quantities of food, if we actually eat mindfully we will eat far less than we would normally do.

More importantly, even while we eat less, we still tend to feel more satisfied than we'd expect normally.

Points to Reflect On

- Choose five activities that could be used as informal mindfulness practice from those you partake in on most days.
- Attempt a few periods of informal meditation. After you do, find out how your mind responded to these practices. Then compare it to how it responds to breathe awareness practices as well.

Notes for Reflection

CHAPTER THREE

WHO AM I? DIAMOND OF SELF.

"What a liberation to realize that "the voice in my head" is not who I am. Who am I then? The one who seeks through the heart finds that stillness, that epicenter sees everything, where "I" disappears!"
~ Yog Nanak

Have You Discovered a "Self" During Your Meditation?

During your periods of meditation, you need to ask yourself if you have found any ever-changing thoughts, sensations and images.

As much as this question hasn't been extensively discussed as a form of mindfulness practice amongst clinicians, advances in neurobiology are starting to air the question amongst biological researchers more often. The teaching shines a light on the "self," as the key insight through which mindfulness practices can help us find virtues such as fulfillment, well-being and happiness.

The "Sense of Self" is how mindfulness practices can change our sense of who we are.

In actuality, mindfulness practices were created and designed to assist us in assuming clarity into the nature of "the self" or to put it more simply, to be precise in how we design or construct a sense of self from one moment to another. As evident from ancient tradition and western cognitive science, regardless of how much we try, we are bound to find sensations and images accompanied by a remarkably persistent narrative when we take time to look into our experiences.

In this context, the "me" or "I" factors of individuality cannot be found.

Therefore, if we take time to practice well enough, we will be able to see that we are not who or what most of us assume ourselves to be.

Identifying With the Self

Self, an aspect of us that is forever constant is the experience of our witness. According to Sufis, this is a center where nothing moves. Sufis engaged in whirling, and in whirling everything moves but at a stagnant center which remains in place. In this instance, other things such as the circumference are ever changing, while the center maintains its static and solitary spot.

Therefore, it is safe to say the journey in locating the "self" and "I," is an experience of an attempt to find the epicenter of self which remains in a specific spot while it watches everything else around it constantly moving.

Karma as a teaching is associated with many eastern cultures and most notably, Indian cultures. It is understood as a subject of incarnation, which is an ideology, wrapped around the notion that how our actions in this life translate into how we will be reborn in the next one. Yet, karma isn't entirely seen as such, and it can be viewed in moment-to-moment intentions.

This goes to say that whatever is reborn in the next life is a definite constellation or attitude in consciousness. Therefore, your intention at one particular point in time affects the perceptions and feelings in the next moment, which in turn, morphs the next moment's reality.

Buddha teaches that reality for each individual is constantly recreated on a moment by moment basis and this further denotes that the continuity of self isn't possible, but an illusion. In reality, what we are left with are frames, with the mind constantly stringing them up, like a movie, into one big narrative.

This concocted narrative is what stares right back at you and gives the impression that you exist. As a result, everything you experience results from this.

A student and colleague of Freud, Carl Jung, gave a similar observation when he spoke on what actually happens when we selectively accept or identify with some mental objects, and reject or decline others. He said that the result of our actions is the formation of a split-off shadow. This is a form of dissociation which involves an attempt to avoid getting hurt.

This got me thinking; since many of us think about ourselves as benevolent, as a result of having a self-concept, your lazy, greedy and dumb side actually becomes your shadow. This means you are bound to have trouble every single time you get into situations that shed light on the facts that you are these three things; lazy, greedy and dumb.

This undoubtedly causes you to traipse through the world around you as ignorant, sourcing for information about what you want to be and what or who you see yourself as being.

A popular form of psychotherapy called "Internal Family Systems," "Mada Dalian Method" and few other similar psychotherapies encourages us to set aside some time so we can attempt to honor, recognize and permit the fears and needs of each of these parts within us. When you can successfully identify or recognize these parts, the parts individually begin to feel safer and calmer and in so doing, don't need much attention to flourish.

Finding it hard to identify with a single sense of self can result in a wide array or degree of flexibility. This is because we don't have to limit ourselves to a particular way, and we can allow ourselves to wallow in diversity and the complexity that comes with it.

Mindfulness practices, such as psychotherapy, are known to become some measure of freeing process where the aim is not to be more than one.

This, in turn, brings some great relief about not having to worry so much about ourselves or how we relate our existence and being to that of others. What we now see and identify with is something greater and larger than us. This identification then goes a long way in our path to well-being.

The Eightfold Path

A host of mindfulness practices implemented in western psychotherapy were borne from Buddhist psychology because Buddhist psychology bears a lot of similarities with that of western psychotherapy. There are similarities between the two because they do not discuss God or Gods in any way or form.

Instead, it functions on the fundamental principle which is the "Pali"term for which is *"ehipassiko"*, meaning *"come and see for yourself "*. Mindfulness practices are best understood by the fact that it is based on what we can discover and not some doctrine. It is a systematic approach and it implores the use of two important systems; *the ability to question authorities and empirical methodology.*

It is safe to say mindfulness is a fan and supporter of open-mindedness because it assists us in taking our thoughts with less rigidity. It bears similitude to scientific posture in this process which we come across in western psychology and psychotherapy. Like western psychotherapy, mindfulness shares the common goal of alleviating suffering.

Other similarities in both systems include; identifying symptoms, prognosis, etiology, and treatment.

The symptom can be referred to as the un-satisfactoriness of all experience, considering the simple fact that the mind births suffering regardless of what is going on around it.

Etiology is seen more or less as our distorted views and notions and the misunderstandings and misgivings we have about reality.

Prognosis, on the other hand, is surprisingly good.

As western psychology circles continue to take up these practices, they often place their primary focus on concentration or focused attention; open monitoring or mindfulness, and acceptable practices such as loving-kindness meditation.

However, in Buddhist traditions, these used to be aspects of a grander treatment plan named the "Eightfold Path". This is structured around "right" concentration, effort, livelihood, mindfulness, action, intentions, and view and speech generally. In this context, *"right"* means *"right,"* in the moral sense, as opposed to wrong.

It is also known to stand for wholesome, optimum, or anything which is most likely to support the alleviation of suffering.

Concentration and mindfulness asides, right effort focuses on bearing the apt degree of control as against letting go or losing control. In the modern context and light, "Right livelihood" means doing work that brings in more good than harm in entirety. There is a level of consciousness about our actions when it comes to "Right action"; this ensures that we reason through everything we do as regards to how it will benefit others, or if it will bring them harm.

Right speech, on the other hand, also involves being aware of what positives or negatives our speech can create or cause.

Right intentions encompass being able to orient ourselves towards our own sanity, and the removal of suffering for others and ourselves as well. Then, there is "Right view," which is about being able to see the world with clarity.

Similarities between Mindfulness Practices and Psychotherapies

Regardless of the endless lists of overlaps and parallels existing between mindfulness practices and psychotherapies, they function in similitude; to drive us in one direction, towards a greater sense of well-being. In recent times, mental health professionals believe that mindfulness might be an element of a central curative in Fmost forms of psychotherapy.

This notion is drawn from the fact that it accomplishes several nearly universal therapeutic goals.

Mindfulness, just like many forms of therapy, seeks to loosen and lessen repression barriers. When we begin to practice mindfulness, certain previously non-existing and unnoticed thoughts and emotions begin to rear their heads.

A degree of awakening falls on us and we become more sensitized to the things ongoing in our mind. During this phase, we become less interested or even distracted by activities we indulge in normally. Our impulses become sharper and our defensive strategies become more visible. This enables us to successfully reintegrate these contents.

Secondly, the manner in which mindfulness assists in the accomplishment of a task deemed to be largely universal in psychotherapy is in the treatment of diseases. The common knowledge surrounding cognitive behavior therapy is to develop and imbibe metacognitive awareness. This majorly means the ability to take note and become aware of what sort of thoughts are rising and coursing through the mind. It particularly focuses on identifying rational thoughts and separating them from irrational ones.

Some Self Reflect on:

- Imagine yourself having a day in which you bear no concerns whatsoever on how others see you. How would this day be different from a typical one for you?

Notes for Reflection

CHAPTER FOUR

RELATIONSHIP BETWEEN ATTENTION AND EMPATHY

"A prerequisite to empathy is simply paying attention to the person in pain."
~ Daniel Goleman

ATTENTION;

We have explained mindfulness to be a form of training in which we build our minds to live and function in the present. In our current age and era, where technological advancements have provided us with partial attention, multitasking tends to distract us from certain feelings we deem to be uncomfortable. It also allows us to feel we can get and achieve more without showing us how disconnected we are.

However, we have full attention when we encounter harm or danger. An example is when we attempt to get a tomato from a bin in partial attention, in difference to when we pay attention while we are slicing it.

Yet, while danger often increases our zeal to be attentive, the intent to pay attention also works like a charm. An example is when we personally decide to turn our full attention to a friend or to a loved one.

Concentration practices also assist in increasing our ability to be attentive. For instance, the constant practice of paying attention to an object goes a long way to help you. At that moment, every time your mind wanders off, you drag it back into attention. We come across these distractions in every facet of our lives, and most notably, during informal practices such as brushing of the teeth.

If we dedicate our full attention to these, they are bound to bring rewards and experiences rather than unwanted obstacles and challenges.

Mindfulness practices assist us in being present in the moment, and as a result, turn up our levels of attention. By assisting us in existing in the present, it helps us stay with the discomfort we otherwise often want to escape from if we paid attention. This way, the muscles of the brain become strong when we simply allow ourselves in "being with" that perceived itch or ache we spoke about earlier.

It also helps in figuring out emotional events as nothing but impersonal uprisings or phenomena. This helps us, not only to grow tolerant but also to be able to exist with our feelings and emotions.

Empathy

In psychotherapy, we have come to understand that others can only be close to us if we can tolerate our feelings and theirs simultaneously.

The Buddhist tradition teaches a means of tolerating these feelings; through noticing not just their impersonality, but by also taking note that everything changes. Instead of constantly attempting to hold unto good actions and shove asides the terrible ones, we ought to be attempting, to develop in our relationship, the ability to radically accept things for what they are.

This means being able to tolerate emotions so you can develop empathy, as it is paramount, if you intend to do so.

Empathy in its own way is a form of attention.

Neurobiologists believe it functions via the action of what they call mirror neurons. A good example is when we watch scary movies; we definitely aren't physically involved in the acts, but our bodies are liable to act and respond as though we are in them personally. This means that the only way we can sense what others are going through is through sensing events ongoing in our bodies.

This means that, having a higher level of inner attunement and the ability to tolerate what is inside of us goes a long way in providing us the capacity to be empathic.

Dr. Sara Lazar stated, in her research, that changes in the brain structure occur with meditation practice. One of these is the Insula. Also, there are parts of the insula that do not shrink with age. It is noteworthy that the insula is pretty much involved in proprioception, which is the ability to feel inner sensations through the body.

If we can successfully feel the ongoing within us, then we can feel that of others or even begin to understand it. This helps us develop "the theory of the mind"; this is the terminology modern psychologists use for the awareness that others don't function or live inside our heads. This translates to the fact that other people have different experiences from you and that you can tune into their experiences and feel what they feel through your own personal experiences.

When it comes to relationships, this is essential.

Another critical element for empathy is Acceptance. Mindfulness practices helps us in growing good levels of acceptance by allowing us to view the judgments of ourselves and that of others as itches and aches, simply coming and going. It comes with clarity not just for how we see others, but also for how we see ourselves.

When we learn to accept our own shortcomings, we become open-minded, accepting others and in return, feel our trust and acceptance.

ACCEPTANCE

In recent times, unlike it was in the old days, the skill of acceptance is vastly gaining ground. This is partly because it is paramount for relationships.

One major way of developing your acceptance skill is to get involved in acceptance practices. One of these acceptance practices is called "Loving-kindness practice". It is an Indian-themed ancient tradition which is designed to enable an open, quivering heart. The image of a mother with a child is often used in this practice.

Regardless of whether the experience is a sorrowful or a good one, they say it is as a mother would feel towards her child departing from home to pursue a profession or get married, or the manner in which a mother would respond to her child being ill or becoming injured. This is what they try to cultivate as an attitude for the heart.

During this practice, emotions such as anger, cynicism and many others might pop up and regardless, we hope to practice the ability to say "yes" to all these emotions since the major goal is to be able to develop profound awareness of present experience with acceptance.

Through research in recent times, loving-kindness has been found to promote positive emotions, as well as act as a resource for a lot of people. Some of these positive emotions include increased feelings of social connectedness. It so happens that it transforms the brain in a manner that correlates with developing more empathy and generosity. This, in turn, shifts us from seeking faults or inconsistencies in others.

Loving-kindness can be related with by those who have good experience in prayer traditions. This is so because both prayer and loving-kindness generate similar feelings.

Although its effects in relation to the theistic and nontheistic have not yet been studied; it is still an interesting area for future dialogue and research.

Points To Reflect On;

- What ways have you found that believing in your thoughts or perspectives can get you in the way of connecting closely with others?

Notes for Reflection

CHAPTER FIVE

THE SCIENCE OF SELF-COMPASSION AND OTHERS

"If you do not love yourself, you cannot love others. You will not be able to love others. If you do not have compassion for yourself, then you are not able to develop compassion for others."
~ Dalai Lama

Clinicians and researchers have discovered a unique kind of empathy essential to any path relating to or with happiness. This entails empathy for suffering, be it for you or unto others, and also the wish or desire to assist another.

This form of empathy is called "Compassion".

Compassion isn't streamlined or limited. It can be for ourselves when we are plighted by suffering or towards others when they are suffering. Research has shown that mindfulness practices generally, as well as focused compassion practices, go a long way in assisting us in developing this ability.

The Evolution of Compassion

Before we can truly understand what compassion is and how it works, we must first revisit its roots through our neurobiology and evolutionary heritage. When we do this, we are bound to realize the existence of three broad motivational systems which are all, essential in survival, in interaction with each other via different means.

The first and the most important is the "fight-of-flight" system

This is centered on threats and is crafted to protect and seek safety. The system comes with the ability to inhibit or activate actions, depending on the conditions involved. Therefore, it can activate us to defend ourselves and fight or choose to flee or cause us to become too paralyzed to move. Certain feelings such as anger, anxiety and disgust at times are activated when the fight-or-flight system is activated.

The second system is the "Achieve/Goal-Seeking" system

This involves a profound sense of drive and excitement, and sometimes, vitality. This is more subtle and is often activate during periods when we seek pleasure. It is often an activating system, and the feelings which get activated with it are those associated with desire and excitement.

The third system is the "Tend-and-befriend" system

This is often found actively in mammals. It basically borders around feelings, contentment, safety, and connection. This system generally comes with soothing feelings and that of relief. It is otherwise known as an affiliate system.

The three aforementioned systems are existent in every mammal and they assist in their survival via one means or another. This is possible because each system is equipped with specific neurotransmitters capable of affecting the brain structures and their actions.

Developing Compassion and Self-Compassion

Compassion as a word is derived from Latin and its Greek translation means *"to suffer with"*. It is, therefore, the unplanned or unconscious desire to help alleviate someone's suffering.

In developing compassion, we cannot begin by developing it within ourselves or for ourselves. This is actually one form of the broader scale of acceptance that is gaining rapid growth and some good interest in the fields of psychotherapy, neuroscience, psychology, and many others. The most interest is centered on understanding how self-compassion impacts our being.

Self-compassion differs in great ways from self-esteem. In difference to self-compassion and self-esteem is subject to narcissistic recalibration; this means that we often compare ourselves to others, who are in some way on the same level as us, and then assume we ought not to be on the same level with them, but on another level.

In difference, self-compassion isn't limited or even bound by these limitations; however, it offers a lot of positive benefits.

For most people, when they plunge into that sense of unholy trinity, a couple of things happen; they begin to feel bad, then begin to see themselves as bad, and then their sense of self begins to take a terrible nosedive. When this happens, the best possible solution is to find a way to readjust the mind into developing self-compassion.

When this happens, we unconsciously cultivate a form of self-kindness.

We don't need to linger in down or negative times; when we feel we are drowning in self-isolation, after experiencing some loss or failure and begin to become more self-absorbed, for too long. Instead, we can turn to mindfulness practices to help channel our attention into moment-to-moment experiences and away from that niggling narrative in the form of "me" and "mine".

Through ample research carried out in the laboratory, it has been established by psychologists that self-compassion is very much different from self-esteem and that it bears no relation with narcissism. In addition to this, it has been tentatively proven that self-compassion is associated with virtually every desirable outcome as regards psychological wellbeing, emotional wellness and being plagued by fewer physical ailments.

When it comes to self-compassion, the drive is to be kind to oneself amidst the pain and suffering.

Practices That Develop Compassion

Through its own existence, mindfulness encourages the development of compassion. Compassion towards oneself is bound to arise when we become open enough to our own suffering. Also, it extends towards others when we begin to truthfully see, through ourselves, that others suffer. By seeing others through our self, and through what is called interconnect-edness, we step out from the "me or I" factor and see how interconnected everything around us is.

Compassion and wisdom are depicted as two wings to a single bird in Buddhist traditions. This means that one cannot function without the other. This also translates to the fact that compassion cannot be effective without the wisdom and know-how to assist those in need of our com-passion.

Mindfulness practices can also be used in developing wisdom. However, in other practices, it can as well be used to develop compassion. Knowing how hard it is to be entirely accessible and understanding of the suffering of others, we usually utilize a stepwise approach.

First Step;

Develop concentration to steady and calm the mind so it would be able to be in tune with what is happening.

Second Step;

Perform loving-kindness practices and meta-practices. This includes wishing others and ourselves well without the necessity to do anything about the situation.

There are some Buddhist traditions that are specifically designed to de-velop and enhance compassion toward others. One of them, the Tonglen which means "giving and taking," is derived from the Tibetan Tradition. The practice in itself is attributed to a Buddhist teacher by the name, Ati-sa, who once resided in India in the eleventh century.

As explained by traditional practice, we exhale goodwill, warmth, and kindness after previously inhaling the sufferings and pains of others. This goes a long way to reverse our instinctual need to battle against emotional upheaval.

It is essential to remember that equanimity is essential in every single one of these practices. It is the component of wisdom and the drive be-hind being able to keep perspective and maintain a stable mind, even in the midst of "being with" someone else's suffering. You can build or develop equanimity by following certain phrases such as;

"Everyone is on his or her own life journey" or "I'm not the cause of others' suffering"

Speaking about compassion without dragging off-topic, we should ask ourselves; what is this compassion which the tend-and-befriend system allows us to experience?

From the Latin and Greek derivation, the first part of the word Pati, which is Latin, means "to suffer," and the second part "com," which is the Greek aspect, means "with". Therefore, it stands as "to suffer with".

Though compassion and love are very close brothers, love is far more complicated because it brings an array of other effects and influences in the forms of sex and eroticism. It also may not necessarily imbibe the virtues that come with equanimity in its processes, like we see in compassion.

Pity, as a matter of fact, is a really interesting feeling.

This is so because when we come across others suffering, we tend to feel pity to or for them. Pity involves a measure or the ability to distance oneself in a way. By doing this, we feel somewhat superior. It is what happens to us when we begin to ascribe reasons or reasoning in subtle condemnation to reasons why people are suffering.

On another hand, we have Altruism.

This is known to be the behavioral part of compassion, and it is often referred to as an important part. This is because, in this phase, there is a wish to truly assist in alleviating or getting rid of other people's suffering.

Scientists through adequate laboratory researchers have found that self-compassion bears a great deal of difference from self-esteem and the two are absolutely unrelated in regards to narcissism. In other words, this has nothing to do with competing with others but has more to do with taking care of oneself during tough conditions.

The research on self-compassion is fast becoming stale and repetitive or redundant because it entails every positive outcome in relation to psychological well-being. It is also associated with other positive factors and feeling such as low anxiety, feeling of less shame, and other generally good levels of emotions as well as physical and health well-being.

There has been ample proof relating the effects of self-compassion with better immune system functioning as well as better heart rate and so on. In regards to kids, especially as it relates to their academics, the positives are endless. It is said that kids who are able to show or practice self-compassion don't easily succumb to paralysis during academic mishap or failure.

Similarly, combat vets also experience the positive effects of self - compassion. I discovered, from my service as Commissioned Officer in the Canadian Armed Force, that soldiers who practice meditations don't undergo serious post-traumatic stress disorders like others who don't really understand how to carry about self-compassion. Vets who practice self-compassion are also known to have improved health behaviors and eating habits.

It is worthy to note that mindfulness itself, in some ways, often tends to encourage and develop compassion. We begin to develop compassion for ourselves when we open up our self to our personal suffering. Furthermore, we can also begin to feel or develop compassion towards others when we acknowledge or begin to see that everyone else undergoes suffering too.

That level of interconnectedness between us is what makes us feel compassion for ourselves and towards others. Taking into consideration, the words of Lennon and McCartney;

"I am he, as you are he, as you are me, and we are all together".

We begin to see this from the moment we will ourselves to step out of that act or position of selfing and choose to see the existence of the interconnectedness of all the things we speak about.

Notes for Reflection

CHAPTER SIX

MODIFYING THE BRAIN STRUCTURE AND FUNCTION

"There is no scientific study more vital to man than the study of his own brain. Our entire view of the universe depends on it."
~Francis Crick

We need to first ask ourselves the most important question; what do we mean by brain structure and function and in what ways does it have anything to do with the mind?

Different relationships have been proposed by varying approaches and many philosophical schools about the constructs existing between the mind and the brain. In this teaching, the mind actually relates with the information being processed and our subjective experience in consciousness from one moment to another, while the brain focuses more on the events around the tissue structures.

You're about to learn how the mind and the brain are interconnected in actions, and how they are capable of causing each other to change in actions and functioning.

Neurobiology; the Study of the Brain

As a result of neurobiological studies, Mindfulness practices have become, often, a source of attraction for people; this is so, not only because they indulge in mindfulness practices to enhance certain aspects of brain functions, but because they also synthesize paths linked with psychological and emotional liberations, as well as changes.

When we take the time to study the relationship between mindfulness and its effect on neurobiology, we become accessible to our mind as an impersonal process. In this manner, we are permitted the opportunity to see that the thoughts and feelings which arise are actually neurobiology simply unraveling.

There is also an array of increasing possibilities in regards to ideas and interventions as is the case of neurofeedback, which is also made possible by neurobiology. In the case of neurofeedback, studies are carried out by attaching a computer to an imaging machine so a subject can be provided with real-time feedback on what his or her brain is doing throughout every moment. This ensures the ability to train the brain effectively in particular ways.

While the processes sound fun and compelling, we should remember that these scientists face a copious amount of challenges when they study the neurobiology of mindfulness practices.

Changes in Brain Function

Quite a lot has been learned about how mindfulness practices affect our brain function, thanks to the assistance of neurobiological researches and findings.

In lieu of this, the first observable change is that of "Attention". These changes in attention encompass a wide array of other factors which are;

- Becoming aware or alert of a stimulus such as a train whistling or a car honking.
- Others include sustained attention which involves following a stimulus over a period of time.

Note that conflicting monitoring, which is characterized by the ability to remain focused in the face of distractions, has been found to be very close and related with sustained attention.

Also, alerting and sustained attention has been found, through ample research, to gain improvement through mindfulness practices. A promising example, observed for as little as eight weeks of training, showed an improvement in the ability to detect unexpected stimuli introduced in the laboratory. There was also a notable improvement to the attention to a stimulus over a period of time.

Other positives are most notably the ability to starve off all sorts of normal cognitive declines which are associated with aging by mindfulness meditation practices. People of old age who spent their lives or a good amount of it meditating are known to outperform age-matched participants during tasks associated with attention. Also, in these kinds of cases, tests of short term memory, executive functioning and speed are carried out.

In relation to the brain, it was observed that varying kinds of meditation practices bring about different results in terms of brain wave patterns or electroencephalogram patterns.

This has prompted researchers in the modern era to make findings on how these different forms of meditation affect the brain differently. What has become clear and known is that effects on neurobiology, as a whole, are measurable in relation to the different practices being carried out.

Mindfulness meditation affects the brain by activating aspects of it that are involved with our emotions; it also has the clinical effect of lessening anxiety by a great deal.

Changes in Brain Structure

There was the now-defunct belief that the brain reaches its peak when the bearer is 25 years in age and that at that point, it begins to deteriorate. This has been conclusively debunked on the basis that the brain bears similarity with the muscle. This translates to the fact that if you indulge it by using it, it will bulk up, and if you don't, the reverse is the case.

A good example is professional musicians have more neuronal cell bodies or gray matter than amateurs in certain regions of their brain and this is directly linked to their musical prowess. Subsequently, amateur musicians have more gray matter than those who don't sing at all. This provides us with undeniable evidence of brain plasticity.

This goes to also stress that what we do with our attention matters and can affect the brain.

For instance, cortical thinning is often associated with aging and pathology; the loss of gray matter in the cortex. Through the analysis of twenty long-term western meditators with an average of nine years of meditation practices, using age-matched controls, in the year 2005, Dr. Sara Lazar made some important discovery.

She discovered that in comparison with these age-matched controls, those who spent years meditating had far thicker anterior insula, prefrontal cortexes, and sensory cortexes. The thickness was also found to be far greater and evident in older participants.

In relation to this, another aspect of the brain discovered to get affected by mindfulness practices is the hypothalamus; it shrinks in states of anxiety, depression, and stress. This is so because it is tasked with emotion regulation, not just learning and memory.

Points to Reflect on;

- In what way have scientists changed their understanding of neuroplasticity over the years, and what does research on the effects on meditation show us in relation to how the brain is developed over time?
- What are the challenging questions that need consideration by scientists studying the effects meditation practices have on the brain?

Notes for Reflection

CHAPTER SEVEN;

SHEDDING A NEW LIGHT ON DEPRESSION AND SADNESS

"There are wounds that never show up on the body, that are deeper and more hurtful than anything that bleeds."
~ J. Krishnamurthy

This chapter is aimed at taking a look into how mindfulness practices can assist us in combating certain psychological issues that affect us in varying degrees. In this chapter, we will be focusing on "Depression".

Comparing Sadness and Depression

It is undeniable that many of us must have given depression some thought and even sadness as well, but never one against the other. It is also safe to assume that many of us have experienced both to an extent in our lives. Did they feel different to you when you experienced them?

Based on research, some say depression has a more lasting effect than sadness. Yet, it is possible for the reverse to be the case, to be sad for lengthy periods of days, as opposed to being depressed for just hours. Therefore, we can say that the length or period of effect isn't what separates the two.

On another note, some deem sadness to be less intense compared to depression. However, we can still experience a little bit of depression and a heightened sense of sadness.

Others say depression comes with hopelessness, and while we cannot completely debunk this, depression often comes with a narrative about the individual and the particular circumstances which ends with the conclusion that things are not well. Therefore, depression can come with a certain "deadened" feel that has little joy accompanying it or no interest in the surrounding world when we feel it.

Sadness, on the other hand, comes with vibrancy and the feeling that the sufferer is alive. It is best described as being poignant.

The most notable difference between the two is actually the manner in which it shuts down the organism or the sufferer trying to avoid pain. While this act of "shut down" isn't entirely common in depression, it is still an important aspect of our psychological distress.

Paying Attention to Present Emotions

There are trivial questions in need of answers when it comes to depression. Such questions might include; how do we work with depression when it surfaces?

The answer is simple; we should learn to focus on the "what," rather than the "why".

Learning to focus on the "what" is basically learning to live with what is happening in the moment and trying to be in tune with it, or attempting to exist in the same phase with what is going on.

By allowing yourself to locate and be in the center of what is going on in your body in a particular moment, mindfulness practices connects disassociated feelings or emotions, which might have been cast aside. This way, it helps us find a solution to the depression we are going through.

There is also an onward growth associated with mindfulness practices when we enable ourselves to ask the right questions such as; what exactly do we feel in our body? What connects us to the pain we are feeling? Is there a way we can feel any ounce of compassion for ourselves?

While many of us attempt to rely on our minds and the thoughts floating around in it as answers to these questions, changes in cognitive science have brought another angle to the scope and vision of this field.

This simply tells us that we cannot trust our thoughts all the time. This is so because our thoughts are susceptible to being influenced by a lot of factors such as our culture, history, and biases in the form of our emotions. This is why with the assistance of mindfulness practices, we are permitted and open to a certain degree of perspective on our thoughts.

This, in turn, assists us in our thoughts which bear features of hopelessness and self-destruction.

How do you do this?

It is easy as pie; think about thinking.

When you think about thinking, you begin to see those thoughts in your head for what they are; thoughts alone. For instance, instead of bearing thoughts about how useless you are; recognize that thought as soon as it edges in your mind or as soon as it exists. This helps you to realize that it is merely a neurological phenomenon coming into effect; that is not you in any way.

Another method of handling this is consciously practicing moving beneath the level of thought.

This will assist you in connecting with certain physical sensations and emotions that exist beneath them. You can constantly practice affective or emotional meteorology to be able to work with this. This is another way to allow yourself key into the Buddhist principle; everything around you is always changing. Therefore, all things are impermanent.

Therefore, when depression begins to kick in and you realize it for what it is, ask yourself, "When in the past did I not feel depressed?"

After this, allow yourself to think about how different your thought patterns were back then. In this phase, allow yourself to simmer with and in the thoughts of how optimistic things were when you weren't depressed; how positive your life was. In this state, we begin to recall all the depressive thoughts and believe that depression was the reason we saw things as negative.

If we are careful enough to take note of these thought patterns, we'll notice the pattern that emerges; that they are ever-changing and never static or remaining the same. The realization that everything is in constant flux debunks the feeling that whatever we are going through will last forever.

Therefore, we should not continue to allow those thoughts to keep us stuck.

Finding Meaning in Dark Places

It is paramount not to limit ourselves from getting into dark places. This is even more essential when we are depressed, or attempting to assist someone struggling from depression. Entering these dark places makes us to connect with and feel our self-hate, loneliness and despair. It, in turn, helps us to see them as nothing but transient. It also helps us learn not to be afraid of them.

We must recognize and learn the truth; surviving this state of despair is possible. Also, we don't have to use it as a tool to cut people off. Most people become toxic when they get depressed. In turn, people begin to avoid them like a plague. In those moments, we forget how beneficial and important connection truly is.

Therefore, I urge you to find "Hope".

Finding hope can be tricky. Most times when we even attempt to offer ourselves or others suffering some measure of hope prematurely, it comes off as failure for us, simply because there is a sense that the person giving such hope lacks understanding of the plight of the depressed person. In fact, the empathic connection provides much more hope in most cases.

While you render hope, try and find meaning too. When you seek meaning, you begin to ask yourself the right questions such as what does the heart truly desires? What matters most to us in our lives? And so on. This is why in a bid to clarify our values, and source a compass for our lives; acceptance and commitment therapy acts as one of the mindfulness-based treatments around.

Through this, we can attain a sense of spiritual or psychological path.

Points to Reflect on;

- Judging from our experiences with sadness and depression at one point in time or the other in our lives, how has sadness been different from depression?

- How have you been affected in relation with when you or some-one you know became depressed? How would you or such a person have experienced this depression if you knew not to believe in the thoughts entirely?

Notes for Reflection

CHAPTER EIGHT;

BECOMING FRIENDS WITH FEAR, WORRY AND ANXIETY

"Self-knowledge is the beginning of the wisdom,
which is ending of the fear."
~ J. Krishnamurthy

Studies have shown that it is easier and more accurate for people with disorders bordering around anxiety to appraise risk than those without anxiety problems. This is because those suffering from anxiety disorders see life as fragile and understand the risk of being alive.

This chapter is scripted to analyze how anxiety comes to be, and the various ways to deal with it.

Anxiety

Three essential and rather basic components of anxiety have been identified by researchers and clinicians.

The first is the *"Psychological Arousal,"* otherwise known as what goes on inside our body when adrenalin, being pumped through the bloodstream, kicks into action.

The second is the *"Cognitive and Emotional Part,"* which is based on what is called a future-oriented thinking, fear and the accurate and inaccurate appraisal of risk factors.

Thirdly, and perhaps the most important one of the three are the behavioral aspects; *"the Avoidance and Rituals"*. These are those things we indulge in when we don't want to feel anxious.

The most notable challenge which anybody working with anxiety needs to figure out is whether the anxiety is noise or if it is a signal. Sometimes fear brings out attention to danger, which necessitates the need to react. However, other times, fear is simply an indicator of what should not be and as such does not require a reaction. The case of the latter is simply noise.

We have to find ways to differentiate, cognitively, between both of them. This is hard because many of us have this natural sense of negative bias which is a deep-seated propensity towards false-positive errors.

Through the help of mindfulness practices, it is easier to spot the base-line of anxiety often occurring in the body and mind. At times, it is the little fears, and at other times might be the bigger fears. With mindfulness practice, we don't look back at the past, we focus on the future and towards the pleasure it will bring.

Some people spend more time looking at the past and in so doing end up suffering depression more than anxiety, while some other people look ahead more often than backward. It is noteworthy that neither of the two actually lives in the present. The mind of the anxious dabbles more in the future and in the fantasies it presents.

Every form of anxiety can be anticipated.

Regardless of who you are, you are bound to worry about the future. Emergency medical technicians say that even those being extracted from accident sites often worry about their future regardless of their circumstance or current condition. They are often found mumbling questions such as "Will my loved ones be fine? Is there the possibility I'd be able to walk again?"

You have to wonder why this happens.

Well, sometimes, people reinforce themselves positively. In so doing, many of us begin to worry and start to concoct novel solutions to our problems. We simply prefer to think and drown ourselves in the positive illusions that will assure us of safety; tell us that we will be fine regardless of what we face.

Avoiding the Risk of Fear or Pain

Due to the fact that we find anxiety to be very disturbing, we often attempt different techniques to avoid the risk of fear or pain.

One of the most common processes is what is called the *"Diver Dan Approach"* to life. This entirely involves a phobia-related method of avoidance and constriction. These are the things we do to avoid occasions or events that might bring us pain or fear or discomfort. In this process, we also have things we do to directly tackle anxiety when it surfaces.

In the current world, many people take medications for anxiety and these medications are often prescription drugs. However, oftentimes, others simply indulge in activities such as watching television, drinking and using drugs. The most common act for curbing anxiety is finding distractions by doing the aforementioned activities.

Through these forms of distractions, we end up developing *"Simulation Tolerance"*. This causes us to want more and demand more doses of what we have been using. This is the ultimate fate of those who attempt to use distraction to hide from their fears, the need for more and more that never ends.

Also, note that many anxiety disorders occur though *"Escape Avoidance Learning"*.

Creating anxiety disorder can be done with easy steps. The first is getting you into a situation. When you do this, the level of anxiety within you automatically rises. Because nobody likes being anxious, we begin to do things to get rid of it. Then we finally find a way to abscond from the situation, and this, in turn, causes the anxiety to abate.

That particular reduction in anxiety is what is known as *"Negative Reinforcement"*. It is a principle that arises when we remove an unwanted or unpleasant experience. This has an underlying effect that you might not even see until you find yourself in another unpleasant situation. When this happens, you begin to seek means to get out of it immediately, or maybe even avoid it totally.

That knowledge that you can avoid anxiety drives you on when you are in situations you don't want to be in.

Essentially, what we ought to learn to do is face our fears head-on. The ideology that we can be free when we face our fears is right in classical behavioral treatment and in mindfulness-oriented treatment.

A heightened sense of anxiety equates to the level of fear and emotion within us as well as our impulses. It is possible for you to be afraid of emotions such as sadness, suppressed or repressed memories, thoughts you don't fancy, anger and many other things. When they begin to air or rise, anxiety comes into play.

Indulging in mindfulness practices allows us to accept and integrate these feelings and impulses so we don't have to fear or avoid them.

Points to Reflect on;

- What is the major difference between feeling anxious and having an anxiety disorder?
- What is the key goal of a mindfulness-oriented approach to working with anxiety?

Notes for Reflection

CHAPTER NINE:

TRANSFORMING CHRONIC PAIN

"The cure for the pain, is in the pain."
~ Rumi

It comes as a shock to both medical practitioners and their patients that research teams indicate that lots of chronic pain disorders, as well as other common medical problems, are not often resultants of sickness or injuries. Instead, they are now found to be results of a complex interaction between the body and the mind.

They, in turn, have realized that mindfulness practices can assist in resolving the challenges. This chapter hopes to shed light on stress-related medical illnesses.

Chronic Back Pain

Through ample research, it has been found out that damage to the spine or the surrounding tissues isn't the primary cause of back pains. Although it is often seen to be an orthopedic problem, evidence now shows that, for a vast majority of people suffering from chronic back pain, it is one of the more occurring and common stress-related medical conditions.

Orthopedic story has explained the most paramount reason for our back pains; evolving from our own evolution from waking on all fours to learning to use just our legs. This they said caused us to adopt all manes of ergonomically unwise walk postures which continues to riddle us with problems.

Though our epidemic chronic back pains resulted from evolutionary accidents, it still has nothing to do with structural damage. Instead, it has everything to do with forces and factors predisposing us towards developing chronic muscle tension.

There is proof through adequate research that structural damages to the spine aren't necessarily the reason for chronic back pain. A study went as far as to indicate that two-thirds of people that have suffered from one kind of back pain to the other had their back pain blamed for some structural abnormality.

Also, little to no abnormalities can be found in millions of individuals riddled by chronic back pain. In addition, there are also people with odd back structures who still suffer gravely from chronic back pain even with the assistance of surgery, which is meant to ease their pain.

This prompts the question of "What could be going wrong?"

Some insight and answers were offered by "Smoking Gun" studies. They stated that a chronic pain endemic is familiar with the industrialized and developed world we now live in. This is different from the developing world, where they are riddled with far lesser instances of chronic back pain. As a result of the amount of money constantly being plummeted into back pain which results into millions of dollars annually, companies are now determined to study who is liable to get it.

An example is Boeing, which analyzed thousands of its employees to know forehand who is likely to develop chronic back pain. Through their research, the most robust prediction that would be responsible for back pain in years to come turned out to be job dissatisfaction.

In addition to this, various studies now take a look at how to quickly get out of acute back pain, rather than the chronic version. The quickest way turned out to be rapid indulgence in exercise.

Some notable disorders associated with the arousal or dis-regulation of the flight-or-fight system discussed in earlier chapters may include; the back, headaches, the neck, other chronic muscle pain, tinnitus, bruxism, eczema, sexual dysfunctions, other skin diseases or other anxiety disorders.

Any of these could easily result from arousal patterns. However, as is often the case, this results because there is a medical component to it, and the arousal component atop of that worsens the condition.

Chronic back pain synthesizes a cycle. This cycle might begin from a very minor injury. If the bearer resides in a country that has cases of a preexisting epidemic of chronic back pain, the individual may then begin to fret about the sensations of pain which will start to emerge and arise from the back.

Then, negative emotions kick into place and bring with them fear, worries, paranoia, all of which affect the back some more. This increases the tension in the muscles and the back pain as the sensation grows with each negative thought.

What Role Does Mindfulness Play?

Mindfulness practices have taught us that pain can be felt as a different entity from suffering and that we shouldn't see impermanence as a curse but as a gift. It also shows us that pain does not last forever but comes and leaves.

In so doing, solid pain can be felt in sequence like frames from a movie. This is because we notice how they change from one moment to another.

It also taught us about the inevitability surrounding pain in life, but that suffering is actually optional. The suffering most of us feel comes from the desire to resist pain and oftentimes, include the acts of wincing and grimacing. Other aversive thoughts such as fear, depression about the situation, wishes for relief and for the pain to end and so on, also accompany this.

According to neurobiological studies, the response you'd get from a meditator is far different from what you will get from a non-meditator if you induce the same amount of pain they are in.

Novices are found to show fewer activities in regions that are associated with proprioception; the art of feeling what is happening on a moment-to-moment basis in your body, while the more experienced meditators show more activity in these affected areas.

This means that they felt lesser pain in areas associated with cognitive appraisal, but more in other regions. Furthermore, this means that the experienced meditator was able to resist the sensations even though he or she felt them more. These experienced meditators also stated that the pain they felt was at lower decibel when compared to what the novices felt.

Cognitive Restructuring

Your level of cognitive flexibility can be greatly enhanced through mindfulness. This is essential because we have to key into the knowledge that beliefs are part of our problems. You have to believe in the power of your thought; how it can actually induce fear into you and in so doing, bring you pain. Mindfulness assists us to recognize this by pointing out the relationship between how we think and how our body reacts.

Mindfulness can also become an important tool in observing pain-related thoughts; therefore, we also can successfully identify anxious thoughts as a huge role player in the disorder. This, in turn, will help us in noticing future-oriented catastrophizing and other budgeting activities.

During commitment and acceptance therapy, we have to find ways to develop what is termed "Creative hopelessness". This is a central paradox in the treatment of psychological disorders as a whole. The order is easily perpetuated through attachment to symptom reduction, or when we attempt to feel better. This is also the case for chronic back pain when we try to avoid the back entirely because we are of the prospect that it will "heal" that way.

This cycle applies to other disorders and isn't just limited to chronic back pain alone.

As a result of our subjection to control addiction, many of us are found to desperately continue to try to get our symptoms or the resulting problem to disappear. In lieu of this, mindfulness practice cautions us and reminds us to control our actions.

Going to the gym is very useful in the case of chronic back pains, but we must also learn to control our sensations. Due to the intermittent appearance and disappearance of our symptoms, it might be difficult for us to control our sensation, giving the cultural bias we have towards symptom relief due to the fact that we are continually being offered medicine to kick the symptoms off.

What you should do is increase your capacity to bear the experience instead of getting rid of it entirely.

Points to Reflect on;

- What misconceptions did medicine have about chronic back pain and other often stress-related pain syndromes in the past?
- What more broadly are psychological disorders, and how do they differ from the conversion disorders that Sigmund Freud studied and treated?

Notes for Reflection

CHAPTER TEN;

OVERCOMING TRAUMAS

"There is no coming to consciousness without pain. People will do anything, no matter how absurd in order to avoid facing their own self. One does not become enlightened by imagining the figures of light but making the darkness conscious."
~ Carl G Yung

Traumatic events evolve from situations which stir up reactions within us that are stronger than what we have the capacity to handle. When this happens, we shove the feelings associated with the experience away. We might even repress or suppress them. However, when we do this, they find ways to manifest as symptoms.

Lots of studies show promise on using mindfulness practices to work through the effects that come with trauma. Considering the vast majority stricken by trauma in both large and smaller concentrations, it comes with relief to know that mindfulness practices can effectively combat them.

Traumatic Experiences

Feeling better through lessening the concentration of unpleasant experiences being felt is the basis upon which many psychiatric interventions are designed. In difference to this, mindfulness practices seek to take another path; to help us increase our ability to take these experiences, instead of reducing the experience or its intensity.

In other words, mindfulness practices ready us for whatever is to come; be it good or bad.

As we know, the most fulfilling and joyous moments of life are often interwoven with experiences of pain and loss. People have different experiences; for some, their experiences are painful and horrendous. Many children have suffered one form of maltreatment or the other, gotten abused, been unloved and so on. This is the same for some adults too.

What many of us don't realize is that these adverse events come with greater levels of incidence than many can begin to fathom.

Causes of Traumatic Events

We are naturally driven into an emergency state when we experience a loss or hurtful event of high magnitude. When this happens, it activates our fight-freeze-or-flight system; this is what many of us end up experiencing an immense form of anxiety. It usually ends up harrowing our awareness of immediate survival.

After this happens, the memories formed in our being cart lots of sensations, cognitions, and emotions in association with the event. Often times, these emotions get triggered and we start to relive them as what we call PTSD and flashbacks, or through painful and intrusive thoughts. The activation of these memories can be spontaneous and never-ending.

When this happens, we are more likely to become angry, anxious and depressed.

The resultant effect of the events might cause us to disbelieve ourselves or change the notions we have about ourselves in relation to our safety or with the future as a whole. Trauma in this manner can absolutely mess up your world. Many of us end up feeling neglected and alone when we fall victim to rape, theft, heart attack and so on.

The frailty of life begins to dawn on us after such events.

When we find ourselves in these situations, many of us attempt to lock our minds and avoid thinking or feeling, through conscious or unconscious efforts. We seek suppression and rejection rather than acceptance.

Some may even find themselves indulging in addictive behaviors or other harmful acts towards others or themselves.

Studies have shown that trauma survivors tend to dissociate, engage in denial or suppression of unwanted thoughts when they use drugs and alcohol in response to traumatic events. Some may even develop intrusive and chronic post-traumatic problems and syndromes because they don't actually understand that these emotions, feelings, and experiences, at large, cannot be successfully repressed.

How to Use Mindfulness Practices to Engage in Therapeutic Exposure

The ability to remain in a place and process of pain or discomfort is increased by mindfulness processes. This is done by seeing emotions as nothing but impersonal events occurring in the mind and body.

Mindfulness practices, through the "Being with" experience, desensitize us from negative experiences and negate the power they might have over us. It does this by ensuring that the traumatized individual experiences less traumatic memories, with lesser judgment and a better understanding of the current experience, with a degree of adjoining acceptance.

This way, it is far less likely that you become overwhelmed by any sense of pain, guilt or even shame.

As we know, when we are less disturbed by memories and don't necessarily have to battle with avoidance, our level of exposure and also our ability to process things psychologically increases. When this happens, we are open to a new and virtuous cycle that helps us integrate the traumatic event.

In so doing, we see thoughts as mere thoughts and out intrusive thoughts as nothing but ordinary sensations, emotions, words, images and so on. This helps us control our anger by understanding that there is no need to be angry. We might even begin to see those previous thoughts, which had been triggered, as "old cassette" and of no consequence.

Above all, we finally decide to stop avoiding or withdrawing.

Traumatic experiences have two main sources associated with distress. They are;

- Just discussing the event itself and the pain it produces, alongside the pain that lingers if we resist processing the feelings associated with the events.
- The suffering associated with attempts to maintain previous models of self, others, and the basis for happiness in the face of intruding reality.

The second difficulty can be solved with the help of mindfulness practices. It does this by helping us understand how our phenomena are in continuous flux and how this will undoubtedly help us recognize the inevitability of the illness, change, aging, and death so we are shock-proof to them. This way, we become more immune to life misfortunes and whatever trauma they bring.

Processing Trauma

Traumas from natural disasters, for many people, are far easier to integrate than those they experience as a result of other people. This is because, with one, nobody can be assigned any blames, while with the other someone can be held or deemed responsible.

This leads us to look at what is called "Dependent Origination," in Buddhist terms. This describes the fact that all things are a consequence of cause and conditions. It translates to mean that every event on earth happens because other events somewhere someplace caused it to happen. This opens our eyes to trauma, be it the ones done by others, or those on a more personal level of occurrence.

From this perspective, we can assign four major steps of working through trauma as the following;

1) Open yourself to the painful emotions and memories
2) Explore the facts of the trauma
3) See it through the lens of dependent origination
4) Develop compassion towards ourselves and those who are involved.

The first two steps border on the level of relative truth and the way we see and conceptualize life in general. In the first two steps, we'd allow ourselves the opportunity to take in all the emotions and further investigate facts associated with the trauma. The third and fourth steps are about transparency.

I'd like to implore us to take a step back to have a look at everything not from our perspective, but as a relation to impersonal factors and forces unfolding around us.

When you do this, time becomes an important aspect, because you must learn not to rush things. Safety is key and paramount when you attempt to treat trauma. Without the individual in need of help feeling safe, it is useless to try to re-join or re-integrate the split-off emotions they have undergone, or to even see them in a new light.

There is also the need to first master and manage your own emotions properly before attempting to do the same with others. Another aspect that is key to this process is "consistency". The need for consistency cannot be overstated. This is so because, without the constant and regular practice to draw from, mindfulness practices become a blunt tool for dealing with such difficult circumstances.

Therefore, our main goal should be successful integration. In this light, we can liken integration on a psychological level to mean health; when emotions or memories are no longer repressed or split, when feelings are still connected and when the body and mind still have that adjoining bridge between them. This is what integration does; it brings a degree of comfort between one and his or herself.

Being a mammal becomes easier than expected, and our sexuality isn't a problem any longer, neither is out aggression, our bodily functions, our instincts or emotions relating to what we have gone through.

You can, therefore, say that this brings a level of spiritual growth; the coming together of who we suppose we are, who we suppose others are, and the world at large. Yet, there is a stumbling block to this; it can only work when a person is willing and ready. Emotions and unwanted feelings are often negated because they were hard to handle at that point in time.

Reiterating safety is paramount; else you will be unable to have stability, which is also essential.

I'd advise you to try a simple integration exercise by the acronym "RAIN"; this stands for "Recognize, Allow, Investigate, Non-identification. This is usable with any trauma-related difficulty, big or small. Different meditation teachers regularly teach this technique to those who need it.

Points to Reflect on:

- What is the determining factor for an experience to be traumatic? State some experiences, whether they are serious or not, which you have personally found to be traumatic.
- At what periods of your life have you needed more safety and stability to handle challenging events? When do you think you might have benefited more from turning toward the sharp points to integrate previously split off mental content?

Notes for Reflection

CHAPTER ELEVEN

INTERRUPTING ADDICTION AND UNDERLYING HABITS

"Addiction is an increasing desire for an act that gives less and less satisfaction."
~ Aldous Huxley

We all have habits we aspire to change, or at least, most of us do. While some of these habits, like eating excessively to handling our phone while walking on the road, are harmless, some are quite obstructive and hindering. These kinds may include alcoholism, substance abuse, compulsive gambling and so on.

In this chapter, you will be taught about a range of addictions and how mindfulness practices can be of great help in curbing them.

Every kind of addiction, regardless of the origin, is built around one particular notion; our hardwired impulse to find pleasure and do away with pain. Oddly, we can actually emancipate ourselves from these habits, but we must be willing to give something in return; some of the things we might consider to be our freedom.

With the assistance of mindfulness practices, we can tentatively see that every one of us is an addict in one way or another. We also note that we are driven by compulsive and automated behaviors. Until we actually pay some attention, they aren't noticeable. And when we do, we begin to realize that we spend the entirety of our day in thoughts about how to enjoy the pleasant side to life and avoid the bitter aspect.

This can be quite subtle.

How does this process actually begin?

Well, the process starts with our inbuilt desires to seek pleasure, as explained earlier. It then begins to take another turn through our thinking disease, because, though we cannot see the future or recall the past, we make plans to maximize the future, which we cannot see, and whatever pain that comes with it.

As much as this is good for survival, when we become successful, a sense of addiction can grow from our efforts being positively affirmed or reinforced.

As OSHO once stated, *"the tendency to hold on to the pleasant, avoid the unpleasant and ignore the neutral experiences are called greed, hatred, and delusion. They are referred to as poisons, unwholesome roots, or fires that control behavior".*

These our hardwired tendencies are what is responsible for a wide range of addictions, and they include ingesting substances in the frame of drugs such as nicotine, cocaine and even becoming mentally imprisoned by compulsion towards any of these.

Some other common compulsive actions include gambling, internet surfing, chatting, video gaming and many more.

How Does One Become Hooked?

Different models have tried to explain why we tend to become hooked on things during the course of our lives. A psychiatrist by the name Edward Khantzan put one popular theory forward and said: *"When we are doing addictive habits, we are actually medicating underlying psychiatric conditions such as anxiety or depression".*

In other words, some activities cure or treat some deeply seated problems.

There is also evidence that some of us bear markers of genetic predispositions towards being addicted to some things. Although, in recent times, most experts claim that we are more likely to learn to become addicts through predictable mechanisms or positive and negative reinforcement.

A clear model proposed by Dr. Judson Brewer speaks of associative learning addictive loops. Drinking, smoking or other forms of addictive behavior becomes associated with positive and negative feelings through positive and negative reinforcements.

When we speak about positive reinforcements, we talk about the pleasurable experience that comes with behaviors in the frame of taking substances; this makes it more likely to become a repetitive behavior, all because it felt good.

Negative reinforcement on the other hand, in the frame of getting drenched by a situation because we are anxious, is actually the removal of painful experiences, that might come with addictive markers or tendencies, which come with the likelihood of repetition.

Good examples of positive reinforcements include feeling high when we take certain drinks, being comical, engaging in sex, or simply linking up and connecting with friends. Negative reinforcements usually involve the depletion or reduction of anxiety, anger, sadness, and other negative and undesirable emotions.

Cues constantly trigger us after we have had one or more encounters with addictive behaviors. These cues may be positive such as beer, candy, chocolate, gambling and so on, while they could be negative in the form of stress, anxiety, loneliness and so on.

When this urge comes through, we basically perform these addictive behaviors. In so doing, whatever unpleasant feeling we might be struggling with, goes away, albeit temporarily. Though at that moment, it might bring a good feeling to us for a little while; it ends up providing us with more positive and negative reinforcement.

When this happens, there is an increase in the likelihood that we will perform these problematic behaviors again. Then we'd have constant repetition and the process becomes automated over a period of time.

Mindfulness versus Conventional Treatments

Conventional treatments aren't known for breaking down or dismantling the addictive loop. In fact, many of them either target the avoidance of positive and negative cues or they target learning to perform certain behaviors which are substitutes to the original addictive actions.

Some of the avoidance cues may be steering clear of gambling spots and liquor stores, which lessens the input into the addictive loop, while some substitute behaviors might be the need to call a friend when the urge to drink comes to circumvent the main addiction problem you are having for some time. This does not mean the underlying craving is affected.

Instead, the alternative is to alter our current relationship to that particular craving. This is precisely what mindfulness practices can assist us with.

In order to combat and kill these cravings, many religious, traditional and philosophical traditions have attempted to implement the use of asceticism, with hopes to separate us from the pain that comes with unrealized desires and furthermore, interrupt the unwholesome habits.

Mindfulness practices can assist us in creating a path towards forging new relationships with our cravings by assisting in the transformation of those desires and cravings plaguing us. Through this, we can learn to accept the ever-morphing experiences, rather than chasing pleasure and attempting to evade pain in a compulsive and relentless manner.

By so doing, there is the added advantage of learning not to attach any form of personal emotions to our relapses. We would no longer see our decline or slip as a problem, but learn to look forward to getting newer opportunities and start anew.

How can we use mindfulness practices to cultivate acceptance of changing experiences, rather than acting compulsively to try and obtain pleasure or rid ourselves of discomfort?

The first step is to take note of the currently occurring sensations in our mind and body. After which we go a step further towards noticing the impulse required to fix it or make our avoidance or escape from it. Their constantly changing nature is easy to spot since these impulses are bound to wax and wane.

Often times, compulsive behaviors come to be because of the beliefs we imbibe within ourselves. Such belief that there is no chance of us actually tolerating the experiences that come with them. With this, we begin to feel prompted to act in order to change it, or we bear the mistaken belief that unwanted experiences will not cease and that they will always exist if we don't do something, mostly to halt them, about them.

Mindfulness practices unveil these thoughts as false and untrue.

In fact, it heightens our ability to bear these experiences, since these compulsive behaviors are designed to lessen the intensity of the unpleasant memories we have or to make sure that we have a pleasant one. We will not be hell-bent on edging towards our compulsive behaviors if we can ride the waves of pleasant and unpleasant experiences.

More so, if we don't do anything to reignite or reenact them, they will not be reinforced both negatively and positively in a continuous manner.

There is a model structured around and dedicated to working with troublesome behaviors and it is called "Individual interviewing".

Individual interviewing is built on the premise that there are different levels of motivation for change for people at any given moment. During this interview, the therapist asks the individual questions relating to his or her addiction, and they may come in the frame of;

- What do you enjoy about it?
- How does it improve your life?
- If you gave it up, what might you lose?

This is a well-known method called "Motivational Interviewing," and it is said to be related to some scientific work on change that began with smoking cessation.

When you work with those with this habit, using this method, the first thing to do is to assess them so you can successfully address their conditions in a stage-based manner. This is done because each method implemented is specific to the type of relationship to the addiction the individual has.

The stage we are, often determines what we might be willing or ready to do. In lieu of this, Prochaska and Diclemente came with a model that has six habit change stages;

The First Stage;

This is the pre-contemplation stage; this is when we don't bear any form of awareness about the possibility of life being improved as a result of changing our behavior.

Second Stage;

This is the contemplation stage; here we can actually perceive and see the problem, but we aren't ready or willing to do anything about it. In this stage, though, we gather some information about what might help.

Third Stage;

This is the preparation stage; here we begin to dive into thoughts about the positives and negatives of taking action.

Fourth Stage;

This is the action stage. Once we decide to take action, we have begun work on changing our behavior.

Fifth Stage;

This is the maintenance stage; it is meant for consolidating changes.

Sixth Stage

This is the termination stage, also known as the last stage. It is known as the termination stage because in the end, we achieve a point where we can no longer miss the habit.

At times, we get to this point and other times, we don't. This is dependent on what the habit is.

There are hosts of programs that use mindfulness practices explicitly to alter our relationship to craving. These programs offer us techniques that are usable by anyone that wants to work on troublesome habits. One of these techniques is the "mindfulness-based Relapse Prevention" technique. It assists those who become free from a habit, so they don't find themselves falling back into it.

The main thrust behind this is to provide us with a new relationship to craving.

Points to Reflect on:

- Name few of your addictive behaviors or habits.
- How can you use mindfulness practices generally, and persuade surfing in particular, to exercise greater choice around these behaviors?

Notes for Reflection

CHAPTER TWELVE

THE NEUROBIOLOGY OF SELF-PREOCCUPATION

"Meditation begins with a call that awakes us out of the coma of self-preoccupation. We are called, we are chosen. Meditation is our response to that call from the deepest center of our awakened consciousness by letting to in meditation we learn how to love."
~ John Mannis

The neurological effects of mindfulness meditation and the various events occurring in the brain when we experience our sense of self, and how mindfulness happens to affect these processes is what we will be taking a good look at in this chapter.

According to discoveries, made by neurobiologists, mindfulness meditation practices seem to train the brain to act in ways encouraged by the world's great wisdom traditions. These practices assist us to shift from our focus; thoughts associated with simply improving things for "me" to allow "ourselves" to become open to the present moment with a good degree of acceptance.

Mindfulness practices bring us happiness. It also allows us to find better ways, through the process, to deal with pain.

Default modes of our brains, as found by researchers, have an appearance in similitude with the mind of wandering. This, in turn, coincides with unhappiness, with activation in a network of the brain and in areas associated with self-referential processing, best referred to as the thinking about "me".

Even though our brains evolve basically to find opportunities and keep away from threats and to sleep, we still aren't doing any. Instead, our brains are often still very much active. During this period of activity, the areas of our brain which have been called the "default mode network", comes back online.

The circuits associated with this default mode network are made up of the "medial prefrontal cortex" and the "posterior cingulate cortex". It is known that these areas are greatly affected by mindfulness practices.

During an in-depth investigation, Dr. Judson and his colleagues were able to investigate that brain activity in experienced meditators and the matched meditation-naïve controls for the meditations, focused on three skills;

- Concentration (refocused attention)
- Open monitoring (Choiceless awareness)
- Loving-kindness practice (which is responsible for cultivating acceptance)

Through their findings, they were able to ascertain that the main nodes of the default mode network were relatively deactivated in experienced meditators across all three meditation types. They believed that the reason behind their result was the task common to the three meditation techniques, as a result of the training of attention away from self-reference and mind wandering, as well as one's forward immediate, moment-to-moment sensory experiences.

This would mean mindfulness has the ability to interject and ability to bring back home "the true nature".

They also noticed certain regional differences in activation patterns. An example is a deactivation in the amygdala; the region of the brain structure that becomes activated when we experience danger during the loving-kindness practice.

This makes a lot of sense because loving-kindness meditation is designed to bring a soothing and comforting feel. We might even have some degree of expectancy, from the practice, in regards to helping us respond neurobiologically as safe and not under threat.

Based on the inspiration amassed from these findings, Dr. Brewer and his colleagues designed and programmed a computer to analyze the brain activation recorded by an MRI machine in real-time. They programmed the computer to focus more on a single locus of the default mode network known as the PPC (Posterior Cingulate Cortex). This is the region most activated by self-referential thinking.

The PCC on the other hand, during meditation, is shown to become deactivated. It is also known as the central hub for the default mode network.

Dr. Brewer and his colleagues programmed the computer to draw spikes in an upward manner on the moving graph when the PCC becomes activated or when it is active and blue spikes in a downward manner when it was inactive. Next, he placed experienced and novice meditators in an fMRI machine so that real-time feedbacks could be watched by the researchers on an available screen.

A close correlation could be seen between what the subjects were experiencing in consciousness and what the moving graph was depicting. The experienced meditators could quiet easily silence the PCC, while the novice meditators struggled to learn how to even get it done. The closeness of how the graph tracked, irrespective of if they were involved or in self-referential, as it judged thinking, amazed the subjects dearly.

Whenever a subject became excited and whenever a subject thought, the computer tracked his or her mind with a red spike, further indicating the activation of PCC.

In difference to an experienced meditator, a novice meditator's graph on the first trial will be filled with a lot of red upward strokes. On the second trial, more blue strokes will be evident but will still be surrounded by red strokes. The third trial is when the graph will show redder and upward strokes, but still with several blue downward spikes interspersed; this indicates that the subject is beginning to get the hang of mindfulness practice.

The fourth trial shows only blue downward lines.

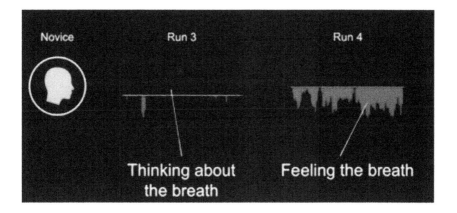

In the case of an experienced meditator, the first trial comes with almost all lengthy blue downward lines, with a single and rather tiny red vertical line. More blue lines are most likely bound to be gotten on the second run, though not lengthy, with few more red strokes. On the third run, we are expected to see the occasional red line.

However, in many instances in the study, we see subjects learning to step out of the self-referential thinking.

Initially, beginning meditators approached the practice as if it is an act of breathing because they were so used to being in the thought stream. Later on, they began to realize that it is about being in the moment-by-moment process of feeling the breath.

For normal non-meditating life, the default mode network is often active during periods of rest. Also, its self-referential processing happens to play an important role in giving us a sense of self and identity.

Studies have also shown that long-term meditators have heightened connectivity across regions of the default mode network.

Through many studies carried out on experienced meditators, there have been conclusive demonstrations to show that activity within the default mode network is more lightly packed and connected with other networks during the state or stage of rest, and in particular with networks associated with attention and executive control.

It is believed amongst researchers that this goes a long way in reflecting the enhanced abilities of the experienced motivators when it comes to being able to detach from distraction, maintain a level of attention, and spend less time mind-wandering, even during periods when they aren't meditating.

In comparison to these findings, those encountered in alzheimer's disease or even in autism, differ greatly. They do so in terms of decreased connectivity inside the default mode network. It is found that in the illnesses mentioned above, there is a relation between the differences in connectivity to clinical symptoms, which involves a great deal of difficulty in focusing.

There are profound implications attached to changes that might occur or be occurring with meditation practice. This, in no small part, owes thanks to the fact that meditation experience is linked with certain changers of similar magnitude which is in opposing direction to alzheimer's and autism.

Buddhist philosophy seems to have paved the way for these neurological findings to follow since they seem to edge in the same direction.

Selfing or the sense of creating a separate self in relation to neurobiology is seen as a key component of suffering. Two types of modes are identified by cognitive researchers when it comes to self-reference. They are the two basic ways of actually experiencing self.

Narrative focus happens to be the first. It is described as that aspect with which we are often engaged, most especially, if we aren't apt or properly trained in the ways of practicing meditation. It entails speaking to ourselves primarily about ourselves.

The second one is known as experiential focus; this borders around empowering others to find their own focus.

As regards the experiential sense of self, it comes off as neutral and distinct in difference to narrative self-reference. It is also known to be a derivative of neutral markers of transient body states. When the activation parts of the insula kick into gear, this occurs.

Non-narrative self-reference and the experiential self-reference, both rely heavily on the feelings ongoing inside of us every minute, through what is called moment-to-moment proprioception. A part of the default mode network which functions through linking subjective experiences over a period of time is called the medial prefrontal cortex. This is also tasked with bearing the memory of self-traits of similar others, future aspirations, as well as reflected self-knowledge.

Researchers at the University of Toronto found that in novices, or those referred to as non-meditators, there is a reduction carried out by experiential focus, as regards self-referential activity in the MPFC.

It was also found that in people who have learned meditation practice, as well as MBSR graduates, experiential focus brings about a pervasive and really marked reduction in activity in the MPFC.

This duly translates into a lesson, from the mindfulness practice, on how to disengage ourselves from the thought stream and subsequently, how to voluntarily mediate or navigate through the experiential mode and the narrative mode. Mindfulness was also deduced and recorded to be a measure of self-report.

When these two are joined, they bear the suggestion that mindfulness, both, brings about the enhanced regulation of our emotional responses and assists the meditators in having more equanimity. These can bring about tremendous and quite visible implications for therapy. Not buying into the self-narrative is characterized as the important section where disregarding or disbelieving our thoughts can bring about psychological freedom.

A neural dissociation exists in the fundamental amount between the two forms of self-awareness. This dissociation is; self-across time; accompanied by narratives with the "me" factor, and the unraveling moment-to-moment experience of the mind or body.

With mindfulness practices, we can see them as distinct and separate, and the clarity of how self is synthesized out of a narrative becomes clear. Previously jumbled streams of information, which we might have regarded as inseparable, can now be differentiated with the assistance of mindfulness practices.

This process assists in objectifying the mind and in so doing ensures that we are able to dis-identify from mental activities as encompassing who we are. There have been records of odd and irregular amygdala function in a consistent manner across several stress-related psychopathologies. This has enhanced and spurred on quite interesting studies on short-term meditation training. Short term meditation training, primarily around one to eight weeks, provided results of decrease in amygdala activities in response to a host of other effective stimuli.

Another enticing aspect of research carried out in the field of neurobiology includes the effects of mindfulness meditation as it relates with the experience of pain. Most of the revelations from this research bear serious practicality and implication regarding how mindfulness meditation can assist in dealing with different kinds of pain.

In detailed reports from experienced meditators, it is revealed that painful stimuli are perceived in a less unpleasant manner when compared to those used as inexperienced control subjects. This was carried out with the degree of meditation experience being inversely proportional to the level of unpleasantness ratings of the subjects.

This goes to depict that there is less unpleasantness being felt when the same heat or shock is applied to meditators than non-meditators.

Also, there are reports of higher tendencies to observe and become non-reactive to pain sensations in experienced meditators than in inexperienced controls. This translates to the fact that experienced meditators have the capacity to feel the pain sensations in a moment-to-moment manner without becoming enraged.

Thirdly, open-monitoring practices in experienced meditators had a rather significant reduction of pain and unpleasantness in difference to what is experienced in novices. This, in turn, means that to obtain benefit from any reduction in the subjective discomfort of pain, a certain level of mindfulness meditation practice has to be obtained.

Fourthly, further research depicted that experienced meditators bear a great deal of decrease in anticipatory pain anxiety when locked in a mindful state. This translates to the fact that experienced people don't get tensed in anticipation of pain that is yet to come to them. This bears some importance because much research has shown that a paramount role is played by becoming tense, which in return makes pain really difficult to bear.

Therefore, mindfulness practices assist in pain by lowering the level of anticipatory pain anxiety. Becoming distracted has also been found to lessen the experience of pain as a whole. Therefore, there is a direct proportionality between a subject's meditation experience and the benefits of dealing with pain.

Through the process of accepting pain sensations, instead of negating or avoiding them, we can learn to tolerate higher amounts or levels of pain stimulation with much lesser distress. This is irrespective of the cause of the pain; medical or "laboratory-induced".

Also, mindfulness practices, through the increased processing of pain sensations, are able to lessen suffering in pain-related anxiety. This is also done through the assistance of cognitive disengagement which enables you to let go of attempts to take charge of whatever sensations you are feeling.

So far, so well, we have looked at things on a neurological level; how experienced meditators open to pain sensations, and how they experience pain more clearly through their struggles to let go of attempts to control these pains. In so doing, they end up experiencing less suffering and discomfort. This is the complete opposite for novices.

Points to Reflect on;

- What is the default network? State the implications for understanding how we construct our sense of self?
- What have neurobiologists learned about how experienced meditators experience and react to pain when compared to inexperienced meditators?

Notes for Reflection

CHAPTER THIRTEEN;

IMPERMANENCE IN LIFE – FACING IT

"It is not impermanence that makes us suffer. What makes us suffer is wanting things to be permanent when they are not."
~Nhat Hanh

This chapter will focus on learning about how mindfulness practices can be used to become more aware of impermanence, and how impermanence relates to greater well-being. Since many of us don't actually focus on death or the prospect of aging, this topic can be a little bit sensitive. Yet, taking time to look at them can be extremely rewarding.

Aging and Challenges, it comes with

We often think about the future and everything it has to offer. We often picture it bringing us some degree of happiness. We cast our minds into the long-term future as regards becoming wealthy, dropping those unwanted weights and even finding affection. This builds fantasies within us that promote happiness, albeit dubious and fake. However, we slowly age and approach the future we were looking towards.

The central legend of Buddhists, in relation to this, addresses the situation. It says that by practicing mindfulness, Buddha discovered that everything is subject to change, and since everything around us is interwoven, then our attempt to hold onto this ever-changing process will only bring us suffering. We end up experiencing this suffering in the current moment because the thoughts, which we wallow in, are not our true reality.

These profound insights are best suited for dealing with aging and falling ill. This is because we are often worried and distressed about thoughts of getting older and falling ill, instead of moment-to-moment thoughts. The thoughts we have about ourselves and about our loved ones is what separates us and cause the life cycle to become unbearable.

With mindfulness practices, we do not recognize these thoughts. We can do this by labeling these thoughts, when they come to our mind, as nothing but thoughts or planning. We can see the thoughts simply go like the clouds in the sky or like smoke filling the air. This way, it becomes clear that they are largely dependent on our feelings and may even affect our feeling states.

When we do this, we see the unreliability in thoughts for ourselves and how they are capable of causing us to suffer.

To deal with these aging and illness thoughts, simply step out of those thoughts and live or practice in the moment. Step away from the fantasies related to aging or illness. This does not stop the thoughts from coming through, but it will help us in enjoying our lives in the current time.

With this, we are left with two major options as regards managing our awareness of impermanence. One is using denial and distraction, which is common amongst people and more preferred, or we can go for practice; identifying with something larger than the "me" and "mine" factors.

The first method or process can be largely unreliable as a solution. This is because reality will continue to threaten us and invade our consciousness. In the process of actually keeping out our realization of illness and aging, we find ourselves getting drained and becoming stressed. How many times can we really reassure ourselves with words, like "I will not have diabetes, I never take sugar?"

This is why there has to be an alternative; to source something larger than the "me" factor. This gives us better options. Mindfulness practices help us indicate and identify these thoughts as nothing but thoughts. It also helps us to identify that there is only moment-to-moment experience unraveling. By doing this, it helps us to see how interwoven things are and how to appreciate impermanence and change.

The Buddhist tradition emphasizes that facing reality is a path to happiness. In lieu of this, they prescribe the "Five subjects for frequent reflection" exercise. Take a moment to reflect on the following.

You can write them down if you want to, and post them in a place you can see it all the time.

"I'm sure to become old. I cannot avoid aging. I'm sure to become sick. I cannot avoid sickness. I'm sure to die. I cannot avoid death. All things dear and beloved to me are subject to change and separation. I'm the owner of my actions. I will become the heir to my actions."

Without doubt, this can be difficult for us to practice, and why? Well, our level of resistance and tendency to be easily distracted or desire to deny, brings more suffering in the end, even though we do it for a purpose. As a result of the difficulty we have in being "with" these experiences, we hold onto these sorts of defenses.

Mindfulness practices come in at this stage to ensure that these perspectives start to take a shift. We cannot neglect how important timing is to this cause, and the fact that there is a purpose for our defenses, even if they bring us unhappiness. Therefore, challenging this prematurely can be disastrous.

You have to know how ready you are, and how stable your life is, before you attempt meditations and impermanence. It might not be the best time for you if your life is currently riddled with challenges. However, if this isn't the case, meditation and impermanence can be the way for you.

Death; Facing it

Death is more difficult to handle or even face than the prospect of aging for some people. Since we are all subject to change, and everything around us isn't left out too, it is often difficult. Yet, isn't it surprising that we are amazed and baffled by the prospect of death? In order to really have a look at this, it is best to take one or two steps back so you can see the bigger picture.

The earth is said to be about 4 to 5 billion years old, and the sun is 4 to 5.7 billion years in age. Whereas, we as humans have only existed for 3 to 5 million years, which is considerably short. By these estimates, in about

200 million years, the earth will become too hot for humans and in an extended 300 million years after that, it will evaporate.

5 billion years from now, the sun will expand to encompass other planets such as Mercury, Venus and maybe, what we now know as earth's orbit. It is also possible for our earth to have attained a wider orbit by then, causing everything to freeze. If this isn't the case, then everything is bound to be vaporized. Or we have chance to move the humanity to another galaxy and find new earth. There is no end to if we keep making projecting. But it may be possible if we see the trajectory of scientific advancement in last 30 years.

Looking from a traditional lens, what this tells us is that earth as we know it, with every single thing within it, will become obliterated. In other words, everyone will die. Yet, isn't it ironic that we struggle to live as if we won't?

While we cower under the unspoken fantasy of immorality with the hopes it will shield us from being connected to one another, it only continues to leave us in a vulnerable state.

We fail to realize that we are just one bit of a bigger order or a larger ecosystem for that matter. We fail to key into the reasoning that we, like other animals and plants, will die. Mindfulness practice assists us in seeing that we are together in this.

Many meditators are actively engaged in hospice work, and some healthcare workers are versed in mindfulness meditation. This is the only way they can understand and be with people who are dying. Mindfulness practices help us, in these cases, to bring forth impermanence. It also enhances our ability to pay attention to death being a real subject and that we don't have to be shaken by its effects.

As a result, we approach the situation of death with much more equanimity.

According to Buddha, the most important meditation practice you can engage in is the mindfulness of death, because it is what can set us free from the preoccupation most of us have with self. It brings us into properly appreciating the current moment. Other thoughts we can revisit during the day include ones in the frame of;

"Death is inevitable, and we don't know when we will die."

Take note of how the remainder of your day becomes affected by this.

You can also picture yourself on your deathbed, surrounded by your loved ones; this image has to be vivid and clear in your head with the underlying message being you saying your goodbyes. It can be disturbing and intense, but this is the reality of things.

When we allow ourselves to explore these practices, we find that we are no longer scared of death. We also find that the fear we had wasn't real, because we haven't experienced it before. Since we know nothing about how it will be or what we can do about dying, isn't it better to take refuge in the moment? By living in the moment, we begin to cast aside many things we fear or are scared of losing.

Also, we begin to make the recollection that we are not alone; we are in this with everyone else. This is what being "alive" means and what it means to be "being". It is very useful to put effort and energy into whatever will assist you in identifying with something larger than yourself. This might be in the form of religious teaching, animals, nature or family and friends.

In Zen tradition, it is said that if one can experience the big death, which is actually letting go of the sense of separate self, it becomes impossible to fear the literal form of death. This is simply because you realize that you have lost nothing. These practices can assist us with the death and illness of others and not just ours alone.

Points to Reflect on:

- In what ways through the period of your life and even in the present, have you found yourself living for the future?
- Spend some time considering the five subjects for frequent reflection found in Buddhist traditions. How will it affect your living today if you were truly aware?

Notes for Reflection

CHAPTER FOURTEEN;

UNDERSTANDING THE SCIENCE OF WISDOM

"To understand yourself is the beginning of wisdom."
~ J. Krishnamurti

There is almost nothing that does not require wisdom in life. It is invaluable for everybody, but it is often noticed in leaders of all forms; whether it is present in or not. In fact, there is an inverse relationship between the notion that one is wise and the notion of actually being wise.

This aspect of the book will take us deeper into understanding the thoughts of psychologists, philosophers and scientists about wisdom, and how mindfulness practices affect it.

What exactly is Wisdom?

Scientists are dabbing into understanding what wisdom is and the parts of the brain structure that supports it.

Do you know that thinking about wisdom and reflecting on your thoughts is known to make you feel a little bit wiser? This is because wisdom involves the ability to maintain a certain perspective towards life and exploring wisdom is the only way to gain this perspective.

Almost every language in the world has a word for 'Wisdom'. This is so because it is the highest human virtue across diversified cultures in the world. It isn't until recent times that the subject became a desire of psychologists and even philosophers. This is because they've always had a difficult time coming to an agreement about what it actually is.

As much as it exists across all cultures, defining it still remains very hard.

Using historical paucity of psychological literature about what wisdom is, scientific psychologists have been forced to start afresh and from the grassroots. This, they did by searching for an operational definition; a manner of identifying what wisdom is and differentiating it from what it is not.

In order to rationalize it, they took two broad approaches; one way is by trying to define it by discovering implicit models, which entail asking people to name wise persons in their mind and listing the characteristics of such individuals of diverse cultures, and secondly, by looking into ancient cultures. This way, they can define quite a lot of perspectives.

Getting ourselves involved in introspective pursuits and the intention to become wiser, go a long way in helping us become wiser. It is, therefore, safe to assume that mindfulness meditation, being involved in arts and also psychotherapy can assist in wisdom.

On the other hand, mindfulness practices help by making us become aware of our reactions to each moment in our lives. It goes on to support us by using our activities as pathways for greater wisdom.

In evidence to this, we look at the neurobiological studies. Psychiatrists such as Thomas Meeks and Dilp Jeste performed factor analysis on the literature about wisdom and discovered the existence of six factors or components. Take note of the overlap in this list and how it has more interpersonal elements than the factors which the experiment Berlin group discovered.

The list includes;

- Prosocial behavior/attitudes
- Social decision making/pragmatic life knowledge
- Emotional homeostasis
- Reflection/Self-understanding
- Value relativism/tolerance
- Acknowledgment/dealing effectively with uncertainty/ambiguity

These six concepts are conceptually related to meditative practices. Furthermore, a strong overlap exists in the neurological changes observed in meditation with three of the wisdom factors or components; emotional homeostasis, prosocial attitudes, and self-reflection/self-understanding. This tells us that the active parts of the brain when we demonstrate these three components are activated during meditation practice.

These findings are rather complex and even regarded as tentative at this point in time. This is so because according to neurobiology, wisdom is perhaps recognized to be our most top-down process. This is because it infuses and pulls nearer many inputs and cognitive faculties. Regardless, the findings indicate that we can become wiser through the help of meditation practices.

Robert Sternberg, the leading research psychologist currently studying wisdom, differentiates between what is called general wisdom and personal wisdom. According to him, personal wisdom has to do with how wisely we can conduct our daily affairs, while interpersonal interactions, in difference to general wisdom, is the display in our thoughts, and the attitude we show towards bigger problems.

He consistently points out that many otherwise wise leaders and thinkers seem to lack personal wisdom. He stated that their personal lives reek of foolishness. A good example is Martin Luther King Jr.; he was widely unfaithful to his spouse and abandoned his family to pursue a sense of enlightenment.

Yes, different interpretation can be given to his actions, since we have no knowledge or understand the larger causes at play. Notably, though it is a sign of wisdom on our part to consider these possibilities, that a person is wise in one area does not mean they will be wise in other aspects.

There might be some degree of enlightenment that overlaps with wisdom a great deal in the form of a construct.

According to Buddhist psychology, wisdom is the sense of awareness of the three marks of existence the *anicca* (impermanence), *dukkha* (unsatisfactoriness) and *anatta* (no enduring, separate self).

Being able to understand the trio listed above is likened to wisdom in Buddhist psychology.

Mindfulness practices are structured to open our eyes and heart to these three marks of existence. Let's have a look into eight skills that mindfulness practices blossoms, which can add to the concept of wisdom. We should not forget that to develop this, we need to carry out formal meditation as well as informal mindfulness practices concurrently.

Step out of the "Thought System"

By paying attention majorly to moment-to-moment sensory experiences, we adopt a perspective on our thought processes. In doing this, we open our minds and eyes to how our thoughts are conditioned by factors such as culture, family and also, how they alter in response to stimuli such as circumstances and mood.

Our intellectual defenses also kick into visible action.

When we make conscious effort to step out of this thought stream, it ends up supporting the ability to entertain multiple perspectives through disbelieving certain unneeded thoughts. There is also the possibility of gaining firsthand insight into how the mind creates what appears to be a stable reality out of the ever-changing flux of experience.

Being with "Discomfort"

To act in the interest of greater good, we must be able to do away with the temptation that comes with the urge for immediate personal comfort. This can only be done when we exist beyond our instinctual habit of finding pleasure and disregarding or shying away from pain. Also, there is a need to identify with our discomfort as being part of "me".

Disengaging from "Automatic Responses"

Regardless of the source of our automatic responses, mindfulness practices assist us in breaking off from them. As a result, we should be able to observe stimulus-response processes in minute detail so we can wholeheartedly experience sensation when it takes form or arises, thoughts or feelings when they occur, as well as have the drive to act in response to it. This is finally followed through by over behavior.

It should be our desire to be able to take the moment to evaluate if, or not, whatever action we are about to take will actually yield desirable results.

Transpersonal "Insight"

This is a direct form of insight into *"anatta"* (separate-self). It is also closely linked to what Buddhists eventually referred to as "emptiness" or "Shunyata".

Mindfulness sheds light on every experience as a state of constant flux. Our minds are programmed to constantly generate words to arrange this flux into what we refer to as conventional reality. This thins and, subsequently, dissolves the barrier between "me" and "mine" and "you" and "yours", resulting in compassion, which is just another cornerstone of wisdom.

Moment-to-Moment Observation of the "Mind's Antics"

This brightens and shines a light on our defenses. In so doing, it creates the possibility of viewing how we see others; however, it becomes more difficult to see them with clarity. But, with mindfulness practices, we will be able to assess and see every facet such as stereotyping, judging, jealousy, denigrating and so on, more clearly.

Seeing How the Mind Creates "Suffering for Itself"

The mind constantly compares and makes judgments; it struggles to project the right amount of accuracy to things, as a result constantly causing them to change. Any attempts to cling unto pleasant moments or cast away difficult ones will fail woefully, thereby resulting in extensive discomfort. All we are open to is the unlikelihood of ever winning.

Embracing "Opposites"

The precious views, such as "I'm stupid," "I'm good," "I'm kind," and so on, which we hold in reality, are basically mental constructions. These views, in relation to others, are easily tolerated with the help of mindfulness practices. Also, as a result of the tolerance gained through mindfulness practices, we can easily find cooperative solutions to conflicts. With the assistance of mindfulness practices, we can easily embrace different levels of reality simultaneously.

Developing Compassion:

Many definitions of wisdom entail compassion and mindfulness practices that show us how we all are interwoven and interconnected. We can learn to live within the environs of our own suffering, albeit with a measure of peace. In the midst of this, we must be able to see that everyone else suffers and spontaneously feel like helping others.

Points to Reflect on:

- What, in your opinion, are the most important qualities of a wise person?
- What gets in the way of your acting wisely often times in your life?

Notes for Reflection

CHAPTER FIFTEEN

UNDERSTANDING THE CONCEPT OF ENLIGHTENMENT

"Enlightenment or awakening is not the creation of a new state of affairs but the recognition of what already is. "
~ Allan Watts

Buddhist teachings have resulted in a significant impact in the west. The teachings continually constitute lots of change in the western psychology, science and culture, as a whole. We will take a look at the potential benefits of mindfulness practices from the perspective of Buddhist traditions.

More accurately, you will be taught how mindfulness practices can help us to bring to life, the psychological freedom, called "Enlightenment", within and around us.

Buddhist Psychology

Buddhist teachings cannot be categorized as a religion in the western culture; instead, they are classified as a 2,500-year-old tradition of introspection, which has evolved into a system for psychological understanding and treatment.

Regardless of this fact, it is still acknowledged as a spiritual practice.

Being able to attend to your experience is possibly one of the oldest practices in humanity. Yet, being able to perform it in an intentional, constructive manner happens to have really deep roots in the religious traditions of India, where it has existed for thousands of years.

An ancient view existed in the time of Buddha; one that is seen in many ancient Hindu texts. This view, in particular, is about conscious awareness and how it is embedded in a sensory system that brings about both pleasurable and painful experience. As we are aware, pleasure cannot last forever, and pain is difficult to handle.

Also, during the time of Buddha, the perception that humans have difficulties and challenges in being able to see themselves and their own world was realized. This created what is called the *"dukkha,"* or dissatisfaction.

Buddhist psychology provides no form of explanation about how this came into existence. In difference to other religious traditions, there is no cause for humankind's predicament, and there is definitely no being in existence to grant comfort or bring salvation. What is left or what exists is the knowledge and understanding that desire and ignorance are the two major causes of suffering, alongside solutions to resolve this problem.

Desire, according to Buddhist tradition, is a tight-knit and deeply seated and situated compulsion to chase after pleasure, and in that process, ignore or neglect pain. During this process, ignorance is carried along in an unconscious and unexamined manner through the nature of our actions, assumptions, and attitudes about the world we live in and who we are in that world.

We should note that together, desire and ignorance morph and give life to how we structure our reality in regards to one moment, unto the next; even while we still try, with limited success, in order to attain satisfaction.

Western cultures believe in reason as a means to govern human nature. This is easily seen in our social philosophy, our psychology and in our system of law. Ancient asian traditions bore a degree of skepticism towards reason. This was because they bore concerns about it being a rationalization for chasing desire.

Their skepticism came with a disbelief in revealed truth, as a result of its wonders, as regards how we know the person got it right. Instead, the major emphasis is made on discovering oneself by virtue of direct experiences. There is also a critic of reason in the west.

Meditation and asceticism were tools used in place of reason by the ancient Indian traditions. A sense of inner query is developed instead of any outer measurement. Asceticism deprives the mind of what it wants, and through this process, we can view the operation of desire with more clarity.

Meditation opens our mind and being to a clearer and even keener observation; it sheds light on processes which normally are too mild or too ubiquitous for us to take note of.

The enlightening power of restraint is the ability to resist whatever urge riddling us for, at least, some period of time. These urges may come in the form of desires to check our phones, drink, or anything entirely. What happens in the moment we resist, sheds light on what is ongoing in our mind at that moment?

Discovery was made in the ancient stages, through the use of asceticism and meditation, that reality isn't entirely clear to us; we often construct it. This is attested to by western cognitive scientists.

Buddhist psychology emphasize on the processes through which this comes to be in moment-to-moment. They give the opinion of the mind as a "word-building" organ which creates order from chaos, and from which or through which we are able to construct our own reality, from the endless streams of data it possesses, at breakneck speed.

They reveal that many of us spend ample time defending illusions and that many of us also attempt to avoid the thoughts of death and illness simply because we are afraid of the subjects. They also revealed the prospect of how we objectify people in order to assume out desires, instead of seeing them as part of a super-organism with whom we participate.

In lieu of this, endless lists and kinds of suffering ensue.

Many of us are blind to certain facts because perception is perceived as a process to achieve an end. We see it as a means of chasing pleasure and neglecting pain altogether. As a result, a level of distortion occurs to our perceptions through our desires.

Also, many of the psychological defenses we portray are borne from our sense of self, rather than instincts. They prevent us from seeing that there is no home and that what exists are the moment-to-moment changing experiences. Yet, these defenses assist us, like we are part of a self-cut from our direct experiences and one another.

Buddha was known to see himself as a physician and mindfulness was his primary healing tool. His instructions were detailed; he loved to number and itemizes his lists to help his followers easily remember his instructions.

Buddha's formula started with mindfulness of the mind, feeling, and body. His initial idea was to start with paying attention, through four different postures, to the body's sensation. These four postures include sitting, standing, walking and lying down. He also brought about the suggestions about being vigilant of the breath and whatever other body sensations arise, as well as paying notice to them when they are and aren't present.

After this suggestion, he also introduced another; mindfulness as a feeling. This majored in the ability to notice if any experience was pleasant, neutral or unpleasant so that distinguishing the feeling response from sensation will be possible. By so doing, the aim of noticing the feeling reactions to images and thoughts as well as the body sensations is made possible.

Buddha's next step was to become mindful of the mind itself. This basically means paying attention to greed, hatred, and delusion, which are things we call the three "poisons, or fires."

Buddha's instructions, on how we should be mindful of all these different contents which arise in our mind, were detailed. His suggestions also bordered around noticing the five hindrances which are aversion, indolence, doubt, restlessness, and sense-desire. The idea is to attempt to identify and observe these elements in the mind when they become present or when they are just arising, when they manifest, as well as when they don't exist.

He further suggested that we should notice five aggregates; perception, consciousness, formations (intentions and dispositions), and materiality (sense contact).

The task here is to note these aggregates as they continue to arise or dim away, notice the lack of any unifying agent in the form of self, sees, feels and also thinks. Rather, a flux of experience exists.

In addition, we are expected to take note of the six sense spheres; how the eyes see, how the ears listen, how the nose smells, how the skin touches, how the tongue tastes, and how the mind perceives or thinks. The task is to be able to note how desire comes to be from each of these senses.

Lastly, Buddha suggested that we should pay attention and notice the seven factors of awakening; investigation present, energy, tranquility, equanimity, mindfulness, joy, and concentration. The task required of us is to note when they are present, rising or when they are absent. In this case, in difference to hindrances, we are working towards growing these factors.

Enlightenment

Enlightenment is brought about by our ability to be mindful of these events in a conscious manner. When Buddha said we will awaken if we follow this course, he meant greed, delusion and hatred will all be cast away. Without doubt, pain and pleasure will remain. The latter doesn't bring about desire for more pleasure, and pain isn't supposed to be met with aversion or resistance.

This is important, so we do not allow ourselves to be caught in addictive or compulsive behaviors oftentimes.

Instead, whoever is awakened responds to events with wisdom and compassion while they emerge. Such a life lacks greed, hatred, and delusion which are all opposites of generosity, kindness and understanding. We should not be mistaken or misled about the prospect of having a smooth sail towards awakening.

In fact, some aspects of awakening involve some aspects of what we might call spiritual materialism. There is this huge tendency, present in us, to weigh ourselves against others. It is noted to be the last neurotic pattern to ebb away before we gain enlightenment.

As we begin our journey through this path, certain thoughts such as "look at how selfless I am," begin to air, and the enlightenment role might begin to intoxicate us. It is very easy to become intoxicated to some of the positive benefits or effects of mindfulness. When this happens, and even get to seek clarity, we seek higher states of consciousness.

Things become worse when we start to feel superior to others whom we deem to be less awake or less aware in comparison to us. We fail to see that the path before us isn't for us to actually arrive at a destination. There is a theme of paradox to this, because as we know, there is a way to awakening, and this is done by being in the moment and accepting what is going on in our *"now"*.

Different aspects of this path are continually emphasized on by Buddhist traditions; using different techniques to try and create the transformation which occurs in the mind. One of these techniques is the mindfulness practice; often considered as the foundational practice.

The path to awakening poses a variety of dangers. For some people, they experience dissolution, aggrandizement or even fragmentation. As a result of these difficulties, some mindfulness practices are rather kept in an esoteric manner.

Sudden awakenings can bring some measure of trouble to those who partake in them without the foundations of maturity. This can most likely occur during meditation practices or in the proximity of a guru or a spiritual leader.

When I met wih OSHO in my early life, i cannot understand what is happeing to me. It took me years to understand this change in myself; in the presence of Master. On the other hand, it is also possible for people to find themselves in trouble with the mania associated with bipolar illness.

The danger of interpreting one's experience through narcissistic means is also a worrying possibility.

Because some of these states can empower the users with energizing feelings and illumination, some people can also become high. Note though, that you can have spiritual awakenings in different kinds of traditions and not grow or move forward. For these set or kind of people, they regress from their enlightened stage, when they get into difficult situations, slowly into a more immature one.

What is missing from Buddhist Psychology as Regards this Path of Enlightenment

Though nuns, monks and even hermits traditionally developed some of these solitary practices in the past, it leaves room for little examination of systemic phenomena, interpersonal skills or even projection. Practitioners weren't often well-prepared through advanced practice for interpersonal life.

Without being able to practice in interpersonal contexts, we are most likely to remain in an unresolved state when it comes to our interpersonal issues. Therefore, it is important for us to cultivate, interpersonal awareness and restraint, by the process of practicing interpersonally, as well as affect tolerance.

When this is done, certain realizations which will manifest may not translate to other realms.

Points to Reflect on:

- State some pitfalls of pursuing mindfulness practice as part of a spiritual path. How have you encountered these said challenges?
- How do you think an enlightened person would act in his or her everyday life? Do you think enlightenment is a thorough going transformation that touches every aspect of a person's life?
- Or, do you suspect that people can be more or less enlightened in different realms at different times?

Notes for Reflection

CHAPTER SIXTEEN

THE ETHICS OF MINDFULNESS

"Now more then ever, we need our mindfulness practice grounded in our higher form of ethics and integrity."
~ **Larry Yang**

In this chapter, we will address the aspect of mindfulness, called *"Ethical Behavior,"* that are ignored in western psychotherapies. We will also learn the reason for its neglect and how it can assist us in becoming more aware and fulfilled.

Performing unethical acts, either in reality or in our fantasies, can transform our actions or infect our behaviors when we pay attention to the entire process. Therefore, being mindful of these moment-on-moment experiences of unethical behavior can aid us in acting with better ethics.

Roles of Ethics in Western and Buddhist Psychologies

According to Buddhist Psychology, ethical training is an important constituent of the Eightfold Path. In fact, it is known as the foundation of a treatment plan upon which well-being is created. In western psychology, these same ethics have been viewed as the province of religious traditions. Using its rather strong ethical focus, "Scientific" psychology distinguishes itself from religion.

Also, ethical structures are seen as a source of psychological distress by most therapists.

Most psychotherapists go the long and rather difficult mile of attempting to assist their patients feel at ease with certain conditions, such as wants, sexual desires, and other impulses of different kinds, that are not allowed or approved of socially. They put in tremendous work to help their clients to not reflect on their own personal inner experiences in a sinful manner.

Therefore, most therapists make it a theme to steer clear of discussions, bordering around ethics, which may cause people to feel less comfortable with certain aspects of their human nature.

When the case becomes extreme, mental health researchers and professionals may inculcate dishonestly, morality and sexual inhibition, and the inability to openly express needs and wants, thereby threatening individual freedom.

Rapid changes are being brought to these positions through challenging research developments. There is the realization of a bilateral relationship between well-being and morality. People, who are found to be happier than others, act more ethically and this translates into more happiness.

Although in Buddhist traditions, people are encouraged to act ethically, some kind of "personal research" approach is being emphasized greatly by contemporary Buddhist psychology.

This bears some similitude to the level of approach which western psychology and psychotherapeutic traditions take. It has more to do with developing those ethics which are derived through empirical means. This means they have been passed down neither from one attitude of "come and see for yourself" or from the attitude of "ehipasiko".

The logic is to critically examine our experience as regards what happens as a result of our ethical actions and what being non-ethical can result into. The goal is to learn for a lifetime, ever-developing and increasing enough moral sensitivity, as well as develop a greater capacity to live in tune with this level of awareness.

The goal is to generally enhance oneself in terms of listening, moral sensitivity, and the capacity to exist and live in alignment with this level of awareness.

In regards to this, it is right to say that the sole understanding, relating to the law of karma in both Hindu and Buddhist traditions, can be found here; since we often see karma as if our good and bad deeds are being monitored by a system, and that this system responds accordingly, either by rewarding us or by punishing us, depending on our ethical or unethical actions.

The law of cause and effect is another view held by the Buddhist traditions. The law of cause and effect affected an observation that we suffer because of certain things we do to others. During this phase, it is thought that others tend to alleviate this suffering. Therefore, we are tasked with finding out which is actually which.

When it comes to Buddhism, morality is just good reality testing manifested through behavioral manifestation. When our visions become clearer, we instantly begin to act in a more ethical manner; clarity brings better ethics.

Deriving Morality Empirically

One way we can do this is by considering certain traditional ethical guidelines. We must be careful to use them as tools of inquiry rather than hard-and-fast rules. We can describe these as "training wheels" at times, and it is used until wisdom and compassion develop enough to guide our actions.

According to the Buddhist tradition, five ethical percepts exist. These percepts also called training guidelines are used for lay practitioners.

Although they are at times treated as prohibitions, many Buddhist traditions see the five percepts as necessary guidelines for a peaceful way of life. They construct a discipline which when followed, brings about calm and focus to the mind and as a result, permits the growth of what has been labeled as moral sensitivity.

The first traditional percept is "Restraint from killing"

Many monks, I am familiar with, have connected with them, attempting to formulate these by pairing restraint and the traditional prohibition with ethical action. It begins with the restraint from killing; the first of the five precepts. This was further expanded to compassionate action, reverence for life, and working to prevent others from killing.

The second precept is "Restrain from stealing"

This is further expanded to mean bearing concern in regards equity and generosity without finding the need to possess what ought to belong to others, and sharing energy, our time and other materialistic things with those who need them. It also entails stopping social injustice through hard work.

The third percept is "Sexual Misconduct"

This is subject to different definitions as a result of differences in varying cultures. However, it majorly refers to skillfulness, which involves a lot of sexual energy, as well as safeguarding the safety and integrity of those involved; couples, individuals and the society at large. It also indicates the need to respect commitments towards one and to others.

The fourth percept is "Restraint from Lying"

This entails making use of sincere ad skillful speech. Note that the right speech is one component of the Eightfold Path. This may include the grooming of loving and endearing speeches.

The fift percept is "Restraint from using Intoxicants"

The positive note to this tells us to be vigilant about our alcohol consumption and to do so in a manner that imbibes and goes along with good health, mentally and physically. This should not be for yourself alone, but for your family and also the society at large. It also entails practicing mindful habits such as drinking and eating, as well as avoiding the intake of toxic substances such as alcohol, and harmful television programs, or discussions.

These ethical precepts are components of a threefold training in the Buddhist tradition. The training demands optimum attention and effort across three fronts; Insight *(pranja)*, moral action *(sila)* and beyond mind *(Samadhi)*. Each one is basically dependent on the other; one brings through the potential of the other two, or the potential the other two bear is in response to one.

A measure of calm and soothing effect comes with performing these percepts and this goes a long way in enhancing our concentration. This heightened concentration, therefore, leads to better insight and as a result, affects our understanding of the ability to embody the moral precepts by deepening and refining it.

Morality practice *(sila)*, helps in developing our understanding while it also functions and acts as an expression of that understanding.

Every single percept provides us with continuity in the ability to constantly practice, learn and attend, with the opportunity of refinement in wisdom and other skillful means. When you practice with the percepts, it comes with the awareness of cause and effects, intentionality with behavior, and reflection.

When you practice, you do it with a light touch. Many of us end up realizing that it is impossible or rather a herculean task to attempt or even succeed in keeping percepts. This goes a long way in grooming and cultivating humility. This is evident because we know deep within that we will most likely fail after committing to the five precepts, yet we cannot allow ourselves to pay attention to what happens.

After each practice, we go a step further towards learning more about the conditions and the outcomes associated with our behavior.

The art of willingness is needed over and over again. It is almost like attempting to simply be in tune with your breath during meditation practice.

How Can Suffering Occur through Ethical Violations?

The realization that violating the five percepts can lead to personal suffering is well known by many people. The different levels of suffering can be arranged from coarse to subtle, depending on the action. The paranoia of external consequences is most likely felt at a coarse level. These may include statements such as *"People will deal with me"* , *"I will get punished when they catch me"*.

On the other hand, a *"little subtle"* experience is what is expected when an ego ideal occurs. Psychologists term this to be an ideal self-image; we begin to see ourselves as bad, uncouth or even worse when we have lust, greed, get angry, or show signs of jealousy.

When it is "more subtle," we notice the suffering of those other than ourselves and feel some measure of empathy or even compassion towards them. In terms of "quite subtle," we notice the stress and tension that comes with chasing our desires since every unethical behavior is driven by chasing our desires.

Examples include killing to taste the feeling of meat, or stealing to derive joy in owning something that shouldn't normally belong to us.

You should pay attention to the fact that anxiety or absence of peace is linked with all these. Meditation, therefore, can be unbearably hurtful after unethical actions have been perpetrated. Eventually, we begin to see that the proceeds of unethical actions aren't in any way lasting or sustaining. We also see that, though it isn't deserved, or transient, it brings disturbance to the mind.

What we observe in most cultural traditions differs from what the empirical approach is all about. This might cause us to feel uncomfortable when we approach ethics with so much value and relativism. In order to solve this, we can take a step back and distance ourselves from the situation to be able to have a better look at things from a vantage point.

When we do this, we realize angles that we humans use to organize ourselves in harmony.

A notion of sin can also be employed, which is what we do most times. We can also make use of this notion in an attempt to get ourselves as well as others to act in ethical manners. Indirectly, problematic behavior has been ascribed to be the endpoint of a chain of events. During this chain, we are encouraged to cry and let out the emotions as a means to bring an end to the unethical behavior as early as possible.

There are sensory experiences, in the form of touching, hearing, tasting, seeing, as well as being able to experience some degree of mental content, at the beginning of this chain. This brings about an increase in the desire to reduce pain and increase pleasure and subsequently causes an increase in the urges we have for some impulses.

When this happens, there is a rise to such behavior.

To be able to attain control over our behavior, we are taught to break through and interject this chain as fast as we can. To a good extent, many of us have been encouraged to limit the manner in which we tempt out sensory inputs. This is actually more prominent around sexuality. In this model, we are taught to glare at others who tickle our sexual fancy and dress to ensure those we don't regard don't become interested in us.

As the chain extends towards the later stage, we seek to interject between the sequence by attempting to clamp down on the drive or whatever impulse after it has risen. This is done as a way of castigating these urges and labeling them as sinful.

Many of us end up learning these first two approaches.

The first approach encourages us to live in fear of some specific stimuli. It causes us to continually experience tension or some level of constriction while we attempt to work to keep perceptions and simulations out of our focus and attention.

The second approach, on the other hand, brings about the fear of not being in control or of losing such control. We find ourselves worried about the possibility of falling or granting the existence of a forbidden impulse, growth in our being. This can cause people to become afraid of every manner of urges, and sexual attraction that is not their desire isn't limited to this phase. Such impulses might be power, status, the drive to lie or steal, and desire for money.

The third approach, in which mindfulness practices can provide some support, is to notice the environment and tentatively accept the stimuli that come with it. It also involves being able to notice and accept the urges that arise in response to those stimuli, but with the condition that we must be able to control whether or not we will act on such urges.

How exactly can we work mindfully with sinful feelings and thoughts?

The first step is to reflect on the manner in which varying cultures tackle a particular problem. When we do this, we are open to recognizing how they strive for moral behavior, without leaving out justice and social harmony.

This, therefore, makes it a practical challenge.

How can we best ensure our won ethical behavior? Is it going to be okay to maintain ethical behavior but also allow ourselves not-so-ethical-seeming sensations, thoughts, feelings and urges into awareness?

These mental contents can be easily accepted with the assistance of mindfulness. The idea is that if we are able to accept these mental contents, the likelihood that we will act on them becomes low or naught.

This happens because, when we get to understand our wishes and identify them as well as reflect on their likely consequences, we are most often not going to be caught off guard. This is something many people are scared of doing because they are afraid that if they permit their minds too much freedom, they might lose the ability to curb their behavior and prevent it from going out of control.

In reality, the reverse is actually the case. We end up, as a result, getting much more freedom of choice.

Points to Reflect on:

- What are the five ethical precepts for lay practitioners in Buddhist traditions? Do they make sense to you as guidelines for living life?
- Which of the precepts do you find most challenging to stick with? What happens in your mind, and in your relationships, when you don't adhere to one or more of them?

Notes for Reflection

CHAPTER SEVENTEEN

HOW MINDFULNESS BRING HAPPINESS

"I believe that the very purpose of human life is to see Happiness."
~ Dalai Lama

The notions purported by ancient wisdom traditions are now being confirmed with the help of a relatively new field of positive psychology. A reliable path leading to well-being does exist, and it is said to be one amidst endless other reasons why it is critical to engage regularly in mindfulness practices.

Pursuit of Happiness

In recent times, focus on researching pathways leading to well-being has evolved through a new field of psychology. From these studies, discoveries were made on how human happiness dovetails remarkably well with what we have learned so far about mindfulness practices.

This field of psychology is called "Clinical Psychology". It developed after World War II with the primary aim of treating wounded soldiers returning home from the battlefield, suffering not physical pain, but mental difficulties. Its main focus was on treating disorders best referred to as paralleled psychiatry.

Martin Seligman, a leading psychologist, after spending years studying depression, in 1998, coined a new term known as *"Positive Psychology"*. It set out to investigate some questions, and one of the very first questions included; what are the ramifications of happiness or well-being? How might it affect our health or our capacity to be effective in our lives?"

With these questions posed, they began making discoveries about happiness being good for our health. Many other Studies backed this up by depicting how beneficial positive mental attitudes are to the brain. They reduce and hinder the risk of the severity of cardiovascular diseases, diabetes, hypertension, cold and so on.

Negative emotions are responsible for predictable cognitive and behavioral patterns in the likeness of limited life activities, but happiness brings the opposite. This is referred to as "the broaden and build model," and it was proposed by Barbara Fredrickson. She made the discovery that happiness has the ability to boost aspects of cognition in great degree, without excluding accuracy, creativity, concentration, and clarity. It also provides support for our ability to play and our connection with others.

There is the guarantee of the right to life is the pursuit of happiness ad liberty brought about by the Declaration of Independence by the United States of America. While this is good news, there is also a pitfall to pursuing life as though it is some kind of fugitive. This is because those who know true happiness have no cause to pursue it or even take some time off to really give it thought.

This is an inverse of the paradox that accompanies many symptoms of psychological distress; what you attempt to resist, eventually persists. Instead, the paradox becomes; what you purse flees. Another way to handle this is to develop the attitude of "let be and let go". This can be learned.

In the same manner our body has points which they abide by as regards our weight, we also have something similar for our happiness. In us, there are specific levels of well-being that we fall back to after one positive or negative experience. There are many things that need to be debunked because many people believe they work whereas they actually do not.

A good example is the notion, carried about by most people, that education, having a high IQ, wealth, and many other absurd things, will bring them more happiness. This is largely false.

According to studies carried out, even being at a young age isn't a guaranteed to bring you more happiness than someone older. Pleasure and indulgence also do not work, as well as status-seeking.

It has become apparent and clear as day to most people that some of these practices can actually cause trouble; without excluding food, sex, power, and drugs. The irony in it is that even something such as achievement, which most people clamor for and believe to be good, can come back to fail us.

Notably, passivity and asceticism, which are the opposite of an achievement orientation, cannot function together. Buddha, therefore, had to source a way of meeting pleasure-seeking and asceticism in the middle. This middle emerges with the need to find a balance between both poles. It is often hard to identify them, and it is easier to make a mistake in either direction.

Positive Psychology

In the process of researching positive psychology, it was found that the activities and various attitudes that mindfulness practices have a way of engendering, work as a means of bringing us joy. It is said to begin with training the mind to be here in the moment.

When we practice the ability to bring our attention to the moment, it further trains the mind into being in the present as well. As a result of the mind being in the present, it can find ways to appreciate these moment-to-moment experience. Scientists attempt to identify the sources of well-being which are not subject to the hedonic treadmill; they are often encountered by savoring, repeatedly.

This simply notices and appreciates what is happening in the moment.

With the assistance of mindfulness practices, we are encouraged to savor and also imbibe the will to continuously let go within us. Without being able to do this, we can get ourselves caught in one of the more comic forms of suffering *"dukkha,"* which is explained to be the tendency for the mind to nag and struggle with satisfaction.

This can be called dukkha of change or impermanence.

The moment our complaints stop, with the right amount of experience amassed, the clarity that it isn't going to last hits us and we begin to complain about that as well.

Mindfulness practices can help us cope with this, because it shows us its fleeting nature, allows it to rise before our eyes and also pass with the knowledge that it is impermanence. Our ability to attain well-being is only possible through the process of knowing how to let go.

A massive shift in the field of positive psychology has ensued in recent years. In the early times, attention was paid mostly on how to experience pleasure and savor it. Currently, engagement is now being valued much more than well-being.

Engagement gets support from mindfulness by bringing a wide array of attention to what is going on in the current moment. It helps us take that needed step away from the thought stream, through the process of letting go of our attachment, and pursuing pleasure, as well as avoiding pain.

Gratitude and Forgiveness

Gratitude is the most powerful invention designed by positive psychologists. By assisting us in supporting gratitude, mindfulness practices help us in appreciating our interwoven states, and in so doing, reduces selfing and ensures that we appreciate others' roles in our good fortune. This is a means of reducing our pride, and preoccupation with it, so we can truly open up and feel gentle and also vulnerable.

Gratitude requires us to have a tender heart and be able to get touched by the caring nature or assistance others render. A good example of this gratitude and its intervention is a gratitude visit. This visit involves writing to someone you feel a sense of gratitude towards, but whom you don't thank enough. This is followed by choosing to visit such a person.

Studies have shown that by doing this, you are not only making people happy to some degree but also making them become less depressed. You can send a letter without having to visit too though; it works.

Forgiveness is a close relative to gratitude. It is known to provide a good amount of freedom. If we are unable to forgive, we bear resentment in our hearts. We need to carry out acts of forgiveness in a thoughtful manner.

In forgiving, we might open ourselves to several pitfalls though; choosing to do away with grudges when we aren't ready can become a big problem. This is because anger has the ability to fester. The shutdown of unresolved emotions causes these emotions to seek expression. Issues can arise when we preach forgiveness to someone who bears no belief that he or she is wrong or that they have done wrong.

This rejection by such a person can become interpreted as a wrong accusation or defamation.

Therefore, timing is important, and when it is done at the proper time, forgiveness can deepen our well-being. Mindfulness practices can provide support in this measure, by enabling us view events via the lens of dependent origination. It does this by seeking information on what factors were responsible for the person's actions.

It also tries to assume the person's role and presence to determine if you will do the same thing in their shoes.

When we understand that our feelings, thoughts, and actions are impersonal occurrences, we begin to see that it is the same for others. As a result, we no longer blame them excessively, but instead, try and understand their situation. Doing this brings us freedom and the ability to open ourselves to relationships in the present.

Meaning and Connection

This has not been subject to the hedonic treadmill; however, it means an engagement for the benefit of something bigger than just us. This is considered a game of win-win, where nobody loses.

Chris Peterson, the founder of the positive psychology movement, stated that almost all the happiness exercises which have been tested and depicted to successful by positive psychologists enhances the feeling of connection between people and others. Ample research into the subject matter has shown that performing acts of altruism or even kindness amplifies happiness.

It is also noted that these acts are more powerful when performed in a single day.

This is just a beginning; if you always push for positive reinforcement and do not give time to understand negative emotions, this positive reinforcement will one day blow on your face like a volcano.

So again, as OSHO said, *"the middle path is very important if you want to have a balanced life. He explains that if you hold the pendulum with force on one side, one day you will lose your strength and it will hit back with force. It also created a guilt of failure if positive reinforcement does not work."*

Positive psychology is a good first step, but for a balanced life, we need to also look at negative emotions and address them.

Points to Reflect on;

- How will you balance your positive and negative emotions in a way that it creates balance in your life?

Notes for Reflection

CHAPTER EIGHTEEN

HOW TO BECOME MINDFUL OF MEDITATION

"When the mind disappears, thoughts disappear. It is not that you become mindless; on the contrary you become mindful. Buddha uses this word 'right mindfulness' millions of times. When the mind disappears, and thoughts disappear you become mindful. You do things — you move, you work, you eat, you sleep, but you are always mindful. The mind is not there, but mindfulness is there. What is mindfulness? It is awareness. It is perfect awareness."
~ OSHO

Since we know that meditation means being aware, whatever actions you take in an aware state is meditation. Simply listening to the noise from within you can be meditation, provided you are fully awake.

When you are able to simply be, not doing; thinking, concentration, contemplations, and become utterly relaxed, you are meditating. If you are able to master this, you will remain in the state as long as you desire; day and night and for months or weeks.

Becoming aware of the way of *"just being"* can leave you undisturbed, and finally get you to be able to do things while you remain alert. This is described as the second part of meditation. First, you must learn how to be, and then learn little actions which may include taking a shower, working, cleaning the floor and so on. However, the essence is to keep you centered.

Once you're able to do these simple things while you meditate in a slow manner, you will be able to develop the strength to carry out other complex things while you are still meditating. This goes to tell us that meditation does not hinder your actions in any way. It also shows you that you can still engage in life and not try to run from it.

Meditation teaches you this by developing you into being the center of the cyclone and becoming the master you ought to be over your thoughts. OSHO teachings below brought me my understanding of Meditation;

The mind is depicted as a shallow state of existence, almost as if you are staring into a mirror you are not inside of, and yet the mirror reflects that which continues to confront it. The mirror happens to be a beautiful and useful one, even though it is too easy to get caught up in it; this is because you are an enigma to yourself, and whatever little understanding you have of yourself was granted to you by your mind.

Therefore, the real you have to be found and known without the assistance of the mirror, and the mind has to play no part in the process. When you are able to face yourself without the assistance of the mind, then the concept of meditation becomes truly known and open to you.

How to become Fully Aware by Putting the Mind Aside

It isn't an easy process right off the bat, but it becomes easier as we begin to experience, often droplets of mindfulness, immense brightening, and transformation. If these drops of mindfulness find their way into your being, then you have tasted something of the reality.

The first step in being aware is paying attention to your body. It is possible for us to slowly become alert about every gesture; once you become aware, you begin to halt things which you were indulging in that bore no profits to you. This way, your body attains a more relaxed and a more attuned state and in the process, a feeling of inner peace, which acts as soothing music to pulsate your body, begins to prevail through your body.

After this, we have to become aware of our thoughts. The same applications for the body have to be applied with thoughts. Considering they are far more subtle than our body, and definitely more volatile and dangerous, we need to be careful with them. Becoming aware of your thoughts ensures that you are able to locate what sort of madness resides in you.

You can take some minutes to do this. Close the door, keep your smartphone away and write. Write everything that comes to your mind. In those writings, you are bound to locate the madness in you. This might be shocking, and even in many cases, most of us deny it is us.

Simply because you aren't aware, this madness can continue to run like an undercurrent and as a result, affect what you do. Therefore the aspect of us which is mad has to be changed, and the madness can only be cast off and cured for what it is, by awareness. For the fact that you can even become aware of it, it is bound to change.

When this happens, the madness begins to disappear, albeit slowly. Then your thoughts begin to take better shape, falling in line, while a deep sense of peace begins to boom and get dominant. With your body and mind attaining peace, you will realize just how attuned they are to each other. A bridge exists between them.

With this newly found peace, you no longer have to run in a different direction. Instead, you become fully aware of your mood, emotions and your feelings in a more collected manner.

The thought layer is very subtle and fragile, as well as difficult, but with this awareness about your thoughts, you have just one more step to go.

A certain degree of more intense awareness becomes needed and this prompts you to begin to reflect on yourself and other elements within you.

Becoming aware of your body ensures that the mind and emotions are focused, since these three are linked in function, like a pulley system, to bring about the fourth, which ordinarily, you cannot accomplish by yourself. It comes to be of its own desire and as a gift from the whole; those who have carried out the three become rewarded.

When we speak of the fourth, we talk about a level of ultimate awareness that awakens us fully. In this stage, you become your own awareness and this causes you to become enlightened or even become a Buddha. We should note that this bliss is unachievable anywhere else unless through this awakening.

Our body is conversant with the tune of happiness; pleasure and the heart definitely know joy and the *(fourth hara below second chakra),* is conversant with bliss.

The goal of *Sannyas* is "Bliss," and becoming a seeker and an awareness is a path towards it.

Since meditation reaches beyond the limitations of time, it is safe to say that time is also mind. The mind is made up of the future, the past but has no experience of the present. It is believed that time has three tenses; present, future, and past.

In respect to this, OSHO does not share any agreement. He believes there are only the past and future tenses, and listening to his discourses will tell you that a projection of the future is done through only one tense; the past.

Present tense is referred to as part of eternity, and it makes it an absolutely different thing. Present tense is virtical in projection, while past and future tenses are horizontal. While the mind exists and lives in a horizontal state, meditation is vertical in nature.

The entire reasoning behind meditation is to assist you in getting rid of past and future.

Misconceptions about Meditation

Meditations don't always turn out right; they can come off in a wrong manner at sometimes. For instance, any meditation that leads you into a deep state of concentration is wrong and will not bring compassion for you. Instead, you will find yourself becoming more withdrawn and closed rather than becoming open.

When you narrow your concentration and try to concentrate on something and yourself, while you successfully negate other existences, you become directed. This directness and pointedness will create a lot of tension for you. This is where the term 'Attention" was coined. It also means tension, and if you pay close attention to the sound of "concentration," you will realize how the word brings you a tense feeling.

As much as we need to use concentration, it isn't meditation. As a result of this, a Buddha isn't a man of concentration. What he does is to use concentration to become aware and when he has done this, his mind gets into the right place and therefore, concentration becomes useless.

To get a better understanding of this, we have to look into introspection.

Firstly, note that thinking isn't the same thing as self-remembering; this is because we are aware of ourselves. There exists a subtle difference which is actually interesting and great.

While Eastern psychology insists on self-remembrance, western psychology insists on introspection. When we introspect, we are more likely to get angry and begin to judge ourselves, as we are forced to start analyzing every step we take.

There is a profound focus on the anger you feel by your consciousness; you simply continue to analyze, work, think, and try to get rid of it as best as you can. The process itself is one of thought. It is one in which you focus your anger to dissect and analyze it. Yet, your attention isn't on yourself at all, but rather on the anger you are feeling.

The only way you can control this anger is through sheer will. This has driven the analytical nature of Eastern Psychology in recent times.

Since Eastern philosophy isn't mediated on anger, you are aware when you are angry, but you don't think, because thinking is a sleeping thing. Though there is no place for awareness, you can be allowed to think you're fast asleep. The thinking process continues even while you don't know it's going on. It occurs while you are sleeping, dreaming or in other actions. Your mind chatters about in a mechanical manner and continues the process in the absence of your realization.

Eastern philosophy also warns us against attempting to analyze anger, however, it preaches awareness. Look at the anger you feel, but its awareness, don't begin to think about it at all because from the moment you do so, you are building a barrier to the anger. When this happens, the thinking will grab hold of it.

With awareness, you are granted the luxury of looking at the anger directly. This OSHO called Self-remembrance. His self-remembrance transforms this anger into its original form, which is peace and love.

When you truly realize that you cannot get angry with people, you attempt to become a friend first before the anger attempts to come through. This form of friendship, which is love and compassion, can turn into anger, and the informative state in which it becomes is compassion. Therefore, it attains its true state through the help of self-remembrance and awareness. This is what we call "Sat Chit Anan," in Sanskrit, which also translates to mean the "true looking and fruit of bliss".

Notes for Reflection

CHAPTER NINETEEN;

SOME BENEFITS OF MEDITATION

"The most beautiful thing we can experience is the mysterious; it is the source of all the true art and science."
~ Albert Einstein

We will be taking a look at four important benefits and what they entail with respect to meditation.

Mental Health Benefits

Meditation practices help regulate mood and anxiety disorders

From conclusion based on over twenty random controlled studies taken from PubMed, PsycInfo, and the Cochrane Databases, which includes the techniques of Meditation, Meditative Prayer, Yoga, Relaxation Response, it was found that mindfulness meditation may be effective to treat anxiety to a similar degree as antidepressant drug therapy.

Mindfulness practices decreases depression

In a study that involved about 400 students (13 ~ 20 years old) conducted at five middle schools in Belgium, Professor Filip Raes came up with the conclusion that

"students who follow an in-class mindfulness program report reduced indications of depression, anxiety and stress up to six months later. Moreover, these students were less likely to develop pronounced depression-like symptoms."

Another study, made with patients with past depression, from the

University of California, concluded that mindfulness meditation has a habit of reducing dysfunctional beliefs and ruminative thinking. Another conclusion made is that mindfulness meditation may be useful ad essential in treating depression *to a similar degree as antidepressant drug therapy.*

Mindfulness meditation helps treat depression in mothers to be

According to findings published in Complementary Therapies in Clinical Practice, based on a University of Michigan Health System pilot feasibility study, high-risk pregnant women who participated in ten-week mindfulness yoga training were said to have seen some degree of significant reductions in depressive symptoms. There was also evidence of more intense bonding between these pregnant women and the babies in their womb. Meditation acutely improves psychomotor vigilance and may decrease sleep need.

According to a research conducted by the University of Kentucky, where patients, which included non-meditators, novice meditators, and experienced meditators were tested on four different conditions: Control (C), Nap (N), Meditation (M) and Sleep Deprivation plus Meditation, meditation provides, to some degree, a short-term performance improvement, even in novice meditators. However, in long term meditators, multiple hours spent in meditation brought about a decline in total sleep time when compared with non-meditating age and sex-matched controls.

There is still debate on if meditation can actually replace a portion of sleep or pay-off sleep debt.

Meditation helps reduce symptoms of panic disorder

In a research published in the American Journal of Psychiatry, twenty-two patients were diagnosed with an anxiety disorder or panic disorder. After being subjected to 3 months of meditation and relaxation training, out of the twenty-two, twenty of them experienced reduced effects of panic and anxiety. These said changes were maintained at follow-up.

Meditation increases grey matter concentration in the brain

An experiment ran by a group of Harvard neuroscientists involved submitting sixteen people to an eight-week mindfulness course, using guided meditations and integration of mindfulness into everyday activities. Sara Lazar, Ph.D., reported the results. She said that at the end of the experiment, MRI scans showed an increase in grey matter concentration in areas of the brain associated with learning and memory, regulating emotions, sense of self, and having perspective. There have also been studies which showed an enhanced hippocampal and frontal volumes of grey matter for long-term meditators.

Meditation can acutely improve psychomotor vigilance and may decrease sleep need

The ample research conducted by the University of Kentucky, by testing participants, which included Non-meditators, novice meditators and experienced meditators on four different conditions such as; Control (C), Nap (N), Meditation (M) and Sleep Deprivation plus Meditation, inferred that meditation provides at least a short-term performance improvement even in novice meditators. In long term meditators, multiple hours spent in meditation are associated with a significant decrease in total sleep time as compared with non-meditating age and sex-matched controls.

Performance Benefits

Meditation gives you mental strength, resilience and emotional intelligence

In the book Wise Mind Open Mind, as reported by Ph.D. psychotherapist, Dr. Ron Alexander states that the process of controlling the mind, through meditation, increases mental strength, resilience, and emotional intelligence.

Meditation improves your focus, attention, and ability to work under stress

A study led by Katherine MacLean of the University of California brought about the suggestion that subjects were more skilled at keeping focus, especially on repetitive and boring tasks, during and after meditation training.

A second study showed that, with only twenty minutes of practice for a day, students were able to improve their performance on tests of cognitive skill. Also, it was found that the meditating group did ten times better in some cases than the non-meditating group. They also performed better on information-processing tasks that were designed to induce deadline stress.

This goes to attest to the fact that meditators have a thicker prefrontal cortex and right anterior insula. It also attests to the effect that meditation might offset the loss of cognitive ability with old age.

Meditation improves information processing and decision-making

Eileen Luders, an assistant professor at the UCLA Laboratory of Neuro Imaging, and other colleagues discovered that long-term meditators have larger amounts of gyrification (the folding of the cortex, which may allow the brain to process information faster) than people who do not meditate. There is the belief amongst scientists that" gyrification" is responsible for ensuring that the brain performs better at processing information, making decisions, forming memories and improving attention.

Meditation makes you stronger against pain

A research group from the University of Montreal exposed thirteen Zen masters and thirteen comparable non-practitioners to equal degrees of painful heat while measuring their brain activity in a functional magnetic resonance imaging (fMRI) scanner. Their discovery highlighted that there was less pain being recorded in the Zen meditation (called zazen) practitioners. In actuality, they reported less pain than the neurological output from the fMRI indicated.

Therefore, even while their brains may be receiving the same amount of pain input, less pain is actually registered in their minds.

Meditation improves learning, memory, and self-awareness

Long-term practice of meditation increases grey-matter density in the areas of the brain associated with learning, memory, self-awareness, compassion, and introspection.

Meditation relieves pain better than morphine

Wake Forest Baptist Medical Centre conducted an experiment on fifteen healthy volunteer's newbies, as they attended four 20-minute classes to learn meditation, focusing on the breath. In the process of this experiment, both before and after meditation training, study participants' brain activity was examined using ASL MRI, while the pain was inflicted on them with heat. Fadel Zeidan, Ph D. , lead author of the study, suggested that it is the first study to show that only a little over an hour of meditation training can dramatically reduce both the experience of pain and pain-related brain activation.

In his words he said;

"We found a big effect – about a 40 percent reduction in pain intensity and a 57 pe reduction in pain unpleasantness. Meditation produced a greater reduction in pain than even morphine or other pain-relieving drugs, which typically reduce pain ratings by about 25 percent".

Meditation helps manage ADHD (Attention Deficit Hyperactivity Disorder)

A study that involved fifty adult ADHD patients, whose result was submitted to MBCT (Mindfulness-based cognitive therapy), bore results that demonstrated reduced hyperactivity, reduced impulsivity and increased "act-with-awareness" skill, contributing to an overall improvement in inattention symptoms.

Meditation increases the ability to keep focus in spite of distractions

An experiment from Emory University, Atlanta, suggested that participants with more meditation experience show heightened connectivity within the brain networks responsible for controlling attention. These neural relationships may be involved in the development of cognitive skills, such as maintaining attention and disengaging from distraction.

More so, the advantages of this practice were observed in a normal state of consciousness during the day, which speaks to the transference of cognitive abilities, "off the cushion," into daily life. There was a focus on the breath in the meditation practice examined.

Mindfulness meditation improves rapid memory recall

According to Catherine Kerr of the *Martinos Center for Biomedical* Imaging and the *Osher Research Centre*, "Mindfulness meditation has been reported to enhance numerous mental abilities, including rapid memory recall. "

Meditation improves your mood and psychological well-being

Researchers from Nottingham Trent University, UK, found that when participants with issues of stress and low mood underwent meditation training, they experienced improvements in psychological well-being.

Meditation prevents you from falling in the trap of multitasking too often

In a research conducted by the University of Washington and the University of Arizona, Human Resource personnel were given 8 weeks of training in either mindfulness meditation or body relaxation techniques. Also, they were given a stressful multitasking test both before and after training. The group of staff that had practiced meditation reported lower levels of stress and showed better memory for the tasks they had performed; they also switched tasks less often and remained focused on tasks longer.

Meditation improves visuospatial processing and working memory

Research has shown that just four sessions of mindfulness meditation training can cause participants to have really improved visuospatial processing, working memory, and executive functioning.

Meditation prepares you to deal with stressful events

All India Institute of Medical Sciences conducted a study with thirty-two adults that had never practiced meditation before. The results showed that if meditation is practiced before a stressful event, the adverse effects of stress were lessened.

Meditation increases awareness of your unconscious mind

A study by researchers from the University of Sussex in the UK found out that people that practice mindfulness meditation experienced a greater pause between unconscious impulses and action, and are also less subject to hypnosis.

Mindfulness meditation fosters creativity

A research from Leiden University (Netherlands) demonstrates that the practice of "open-monitoring" meditation (non-reactively monitoring the content of experience from moment-to-moment) has positive effects in creativity and divergent thinking. Participants who had followed the practice performed better when asked to creatively come up with new ideas.

Physical Benefits

Meditation reduces the risk of heart diseases and stroke

Heart diseases and stroke are primary sources of death around the world.

According to a study published in late 2012, a group of over 200 high-risk individuals were given the options of either taking a health education class promoting better diet and exercise or taking a class on Transcendental Meditation. During the next 5 years, researchers found that those who took the meditation class had a 48% reduction in their overall risk of heart attack, stroke, and death. They noted that meditation *"significantly reduced risk for mortality, myocardial infarction, and stroke in coronary heart disease patients. These changes were associated with lower blood pressure and psychosocial stress factors"*.

Meditation affects genes that control stress and immunity

A study from Harvard Medical School demonstrates that, after practicing yoga and meditation, the individuals had improved mitochondrial energy production, consumption, and resiliency. This improvement develops a higher immunity and resilience to stress in the system.

Meditation reduces blood pressure

Clinical research has demonstrated that the practice of Zen Meditation (also known as "Zazen") reduces stress and high blood pressure. Another experiment using a technique called "relaxation response," yielded similar results; 2/3 of high blood pressure patients showed significant drops in blood pressure after 3 months of meditation, which consequently meant less need for medication. This is because relaxation results in the formation of nitric oxide opens up the blood vessels.

Mindfulness training decreases inflammatory disorders

A study conducted in France and Spain at the UW-Madison Waisman Centre discovered that the practice of mindfulness meditation produced a range of genetic and molecular effects on the participants. More specifically, it noted reduced levels of pro-inflammatory genes, which in turn correlated with faster physical recovery from a stressful situation.

Mindfulness practice helps prevent asthma, rheumatoid arthritis, and inflammatory bowel disease

In a research conducted by neuroscientists of the University of Wisconsin-Madison, two groups of people were exposed to different methods of stress control. One of them received mindfulness training, while the other received nutritional education, exercise, and music therapy. The study concluded that mindfulness techniques were more effective in relieving inflammatory symptoms than other activities that promote well-being.

Mindfulness meditation reduces risk of Alzheimer's and premature death

Results from recent research, published online in the journal *Brain, Behavior and Immunity*, states that just 30 minutes of meditation a day not only reduces the sense of loneliness but also reduces the risk of heart disease, depression, Alzheimer's and premature death.

Mindfulness training is helpful for patients diagnosed with

Fibromyalgia

In a study published in PubMed, 11 participants that suffered from Fibromyalgia underwent 8-week mindfulness training. The researchers found significant improvement in the overall health status of the participants and in symptoms of stiffness, anxiety, and depression. Significant improvements were also seen in the reported number of days they "felt well" and number of days they "missed work" because of Fibromyalgia.

Meditation helps manage the heart rate and respiratory rate

In a study published by the Korean Association of Genuine Traditional Medicine, practitioners of "Integrated Amrita Meditation Technique" showed a significant decrease in heart rate and respiratory rate for up to 8 months after the training period.

Mindfulness meditation may even help treat HIV

Quoting from a study from UCLA:

"Lymphocytes, or simply CD4 T cells, are the "brains" of the immune system, coordinating its activity when the body comes under attack. They are also the cells that are attacked by HIV, the devastating virus that causes AIDS and has infected roughly 40 million people worldwide. The virus slowly eats away at CD4 T cells, weakening the immune system.

But the immune systems of HIV/AIDS patients face another enemy as well – stress, which can accelerate CD4 T cell declines. Now, researchers at UCLA report that the practice of mindfulness meditation stopped the decline of CD4 T cells in HIV-positive patients suffering from stress, slowing the progression of the disease. "

Creswell and his colleagues ran an eight-week mindfulness-based stress-reduction (MBSR) meditation program and compared it to a one-day MBSR control seminar using a stressed and ethnically diverse sample of 48 HIV-positive adults in Los Angeles. Participants in the eight-week group showed no loss of CD4 T cells, indicating that mindfulness meditation training can buffer declines. In contrast, the control group showed significant declines in CD4 T cells from pre-study to post-study. Such declines are a characteristic hallmark of HIV progression.

Meditation may make you live longer

Telomeres are an essential part of human cells that affect how our cells age. Though the research is not conclusive yet, there is data suggesting that *"some forms of meditation may have salutary effects on telomere length by reducing cognitive stress and stress arousal and increasing positive states of mind and hormonal factors that may promote telomere maintenance.* "

Meditation helps manage psoriasis

Psychological stress is a potent trigger of inflammation. A brief mindfulness meditation-based stress reduction intervention, delivered by audiotape during ultraviolet light therapy, was found to increase the resolution of psoriatic lesions in patients with psoriasis.

Thanks to the reader Maricarmen for pointing out this fact.

Relationship Benefits

Mindfulness meditation decreases feelings of loneliness

A study from Carnegie Mellon University indicates that mindfulness meditation training is useful in decreasing feelings of loneliness, which in turn decreases the risk for morbidity, mortality, and expression of pro-inflammatory genes.

Meditation increases feelings of compassion and decreases worry

After being assigned to a 9-week compassion cultivation training

(CCT), individuals showed significant improvements in all three domains of compassion – compassion for others, receiving compassion from others, and self-compassion. In a similar situation, the practitioners also experienced decreased levels of worry and emotional suppression.

Loving-kindness meditation improves empathy and positive relationships

In Buddhist traditions, the practice of loving-kindness or *metta* exists where the practitioner focuses on being able to develop a sense of benevolence and care towards every living thing.

According to a study from *Emory University*, such exercises effectively boost one's ability to empathize with others by way of reading their facial expressions. Another study points out that the development of positive emotions through compassion builds up several personal resources, including *"a loving attitude towards oneself and others, and includes self-acceptance, social support received, and positive relations with others," as well as "feeling of competence about one's life" and includes "pathways thinking environmental mastery, purpose in life, and ego-resilience."*

Loving-kindness meditation also reduces social isolation

In a study published in the American Psychological Association, subjects that did "even just a few minutes of loving-kindness meditation increased feelings of social connection and positivity toward novel individuals, on both explicit and implicit levels. These results suggest that this easily implemented technique may help to increase positive social emotions and decrease social isolation".

Notes for Reflection

CHAPTER TWENTY

WHERE TO FIND ONLINE AND RETREAT CENTERS FOR MEDITATION

"There is no other miracle in the world then meditation. It is the only science of transformation."
~ OSHO

There are many locations around the world for meditation. But from my experience, if you really need a change, an environment where you can be protected and provided full support is OSHO INTERNATIONAL MEDITATION RESORT. This is the place I lived with OSHO and experienced personal transformation in the presence of Master. Below is the information on this great retreat center.

There are also other meditation centers that are run by senior OSHO disciples like Nisarga OSHO in Himachal Parades, India: OSHO Dham in New Delhi, OSHO Tapoban in Nepal and many more.

OSHO International Meditation Resort

Each year the Meditation Resort welcomes thousands of people from more than 100 countries. This unique campus provides an opportunity for the direct experience of the new way of living with more awareness, relaxation, celebration, and creativity. A great variety of around-the-clock and around-the-year program options are available. Doing nothing and just relaxing is one of them!

All the programs are based on the Osho's vision of "Zorba the Buddha" a qualitative new kind of human being that is able to participate both in creativity of everyday life and relax into the silence and meditation.

Location

100 miles southeast of Mumbai (Bombay) in the thriving modern city of Pune, India, the OSHO International Meditation Resort is a holiday destination with a difference.

The meditation Resort is spread over 29 acres of spectacular gardens in the beautiful tree-lined residential area.

OSHO Meditations

A full daily schedule of meditation for every type of person includes both the traditional and revolutionary methods and the OSHO Active Meditations. The daily meditation program takes place in what must be the world's largest meditation hall; the OSHO Auditorium.

OSHO Multiversity

For Individual sessions, courses and workshops cover everything from creative arts to holistic health, personal transformation, relationship, and life transition, transformation meditation into a lifestyle for life and work, esoteric science, and the "Zen" approach to sports and recreation. The secret of the OSHO Multiversity's success lies in the fact that all its programs are combined with meditation, supporting the understanding that, as human beings, we are far more than the sum of the parts.

Cuisine

A variety of different eating areas serve delicious western Asian and Indian vegetarian food – most of it is organically grown especially for the Meditation Resort. Breads and cakes are baked in the resort's own bakery.

Night Life:

There are many evening events to choose from – dancing being at the top of the list! Other activities include full-moon meditations beneath the stars, variety shows, music performances and meditations for daily life.

Facilities:

You can buy all your basic necessities and toiletry in the Galleria. The multimedia gallery sells a large range of OSHO media products. There is a bank, a travel agency, and a Cyber Café on campus. For those who enjoy shopping, Pune provides all the options, ranging from traditional and ethnic Indian products to all the global brand name stores.

Accommodation

You can choose to stay in the elegant rooms of the OSHO Guesthouse, or, for longer stays on the campus, you can select one of the OSHO Living-in-program. Additionally, there is a plentiful variety of nearby hotels and serviced apartments.

Meditation Resort : www. osho. com/meditaitonresort

Guesthouse : www. osho. com/guesthouse

Living in Program: www. osho. com/livingin

OSOH Active Meditation: www. osho. com/meditate

iOSHO : https://www. osho. com/iosho/zen-tarot/paradox

OSHO Newsletter: https://www. osho. com/read/newsletters/subscribe

OSHO on Facebook: https://www. facebook. com/osho. international/

If you have any question feel free to connect with me on facebook and linkedin.

https://www.facebook.com/ozenlearning

https://www.linkedin.com/in/sohal/

Thanks for buying this book!

Made in the USA
Monee, IL
09 March 2020